Educating Leaders for Ministry

Issues and Responses

Victor J. Klimoski

Kevin J. O'Neil, C.Ss.R.

Katarina M. Schuth, O.S.F.

Commentary

Thomas Esselman, C.M.

Jeanne McLean, Ph.D.

Donald Senior, C.P.

A Michael Glazier Book

LITURGICAL PRESS

Collegeville, Minnesota

www.litpress.org

A Michael Glazier book published by Liturgical Press.

Cover design by David Manahan, O.S.B. Illustration provided by Banana Stock Photos.

Scripture texts used in this work are taken from the *New American Bible* © 1970 Confraternity of Christian Doctrine, Washington, D.C., and are used by permission of the copyright owner. All rights reserved. No part of the *New American Bible* may be reproduced in any form without permission in writing from the copyright owner.

1   2   3   4   5   6   7   8

Library of Congress Cataloging-in-Publication Data

Klimoski, Victor J.
    Educating leaders for ministry : issues and responses / Victor J. Klimoski, Kevin J. O'Neil, Katarina M. Schuth.
      p. cm.
    "A Michael Glazier book."
    Summary: "Draws principally on a project entitled 'Theological Teaching for the Church's Ministries' (also called the 'Keystone Conferences') and names four overarching challenges in theological education: theological differences, learning differences, integration, and assessment"—Provided by publisher.
    Includes bibliographical references and index.
    ISBN-13: 978-0-8146-5183-4 (pbk. : alk. paper)
    ISBN-10: 0-8146-5183-6 (pbk. : alk. paper)
    1. Theology—Study and teaching.   2. Christian leadership.   3. Pastoral theology. I. O'Neil, Kevin, 1955–   II. Schuth, Katarina.   III. Title.

BV4020.K55 2005
230'.071'1—dc22

2005004343

Contents

— Commentary —

Thomas Esselman, C.M.
Associate Professor of Systemic Theology
Aquinas Institute of Theology, St. Louis, Missouri

Jeanne McLean, Ph.D.
Dean, The Saint Paul Seminary School of Divinity
University of St. Thomas

Donald Senior, C.P.
President, Catholic Theological Union, Chicago

Mary C. Boys, S.N.J.M.
Kathy Brown
Bishop Ricardo Ramirez, C.S.B.
Peter Steinfels
Barry Strong, O.S.F.S.
Raymond Williams

Foreword

Educators are coming to the realization that their work is more about learning than teaching. While teaching is a constituent element in any good education, it is the *process* of teaching that has reformulated the calculus of education. Process involves the awareness of students' cultural backgrounds, the recognition of the experiential as well as the cognitional, and the evaluation of whether real learning actually occurred. All this places an emphasis squarely on learning. Nowhere is this more relevant than in graduate theological schools for ministry in the United States. Ministry, of its nature, is a learned art that embraces the entirety of the practitioner's life. When schools focus on theology and ministry in service to the Church, the importance of cultivating lifelong disciplines of learning emerges with special clarity.

It was with such an awareness about teaching and learning that a group of Catholic theological educators, the Lilly Endowment Inc., and the Franciscan Friars of Holy Name Province provided annual conferences from 1995 to 2001 for theological faculty teams to discuss, think about, and reformulate the enterprise of Catholic education and formation for ministry. During that period twenty Catholic schools of theology developed case studies, explored them in group discussion, and engaged in guided reflection to uncover a "common wisdom" that could be evaluated, assessed, and shared with professional colleagues in theological education.

The findings of those six years of disciplined conversation are the material of this volume. They reflect the best thinking of what we learned. The authors seek to spark thoughtful discussion within the entire community of theological educators throughout the United States about what education for ministry entails in this changing and complex society and in the larger world we inhabit. Segments might seem particularly slanted for Catholic educators, but much of the book is applicable to theological education across denominations and religions.

I also believe that this material serves a secondary but related audience: the local congregation. This is because a central thrust of the book calls for an informed and nuanced reading of the groups we serve. As a result, insights into adult learning apply both to seminary classroom and to parish pulpit and adult education forum. In the robust, pluralistic climate of this country, the volume serves as a valuable handbook.

The authors and commentators are indeed experts in their fields. Their contributions reflect what they heard and learned as a result of the project and in light of their own experience. They then formulated what seemed most useful for fostering effective theological education designed to prepare men and women for professional ministry. The task of putting this learning together was not an easy one but results from prolonged discussion and careful critique. I believe the effort expands our understanding and provides practical applications for the work of preparing people for ministerial leadership. The authors also try to bridge the world of the theological school and the parish, offering ways in which key themes and responses emerging from the Conferences might be helpful in parish life.

These chapters are offered not as the last word, but as the *first* word. The hope is that this gathering of wisdom will spark rich and fruitful conversations among faculty, students, board, and President/Rector as to what theological education for ministry entails as we begin the twenty-first century. I am pleased to invite you into this larger, ongoing conversation with the hope that it will stimulate your own thinking about this vital area of mission and service.

Vincent Cushing, O.F.M.
President Emeritus and Professor of Systematic Theology
Washington Theological Union

Acknowledgments

We are indebted to many people who supported and participated in the Keystone Conferences. Their work provided the material for this volume. We owe a particular debt of gratitude to Rev. Vincent Cushing, O.F.M., Mr. Fred Hofheinz, and Dr. Christa Klein who, with Sr. Katarina Schuth, O.S.F., are the principal architects of the Keystone Conferences. The Conferences and this book would not have been possible without the generosity of the Lilly Endowment Inc. and more importantly the active support of Fred Hofheinz, former program director for religion, John Wimmer, who succeeded him in that role, and Craig Dykstra, who is vice-president of the religion division at the Endowment. The Franciscan Friars of the Holy Name Province, administrators of the Bonfils-Stanton Trust, provided additional financial support that was indispensable and for which we are very grateful. Grants for this project were administered by the Washington Theological Union whose past president, Rev. Vincent Cushing, O.F.M., and current president, Rev. Daniel McClellan, O.F.M., were generous in their encouragement and promotion of project goals.

We thank Nancy Steckel, Alyce Korba, and Catherine Slight whose administrative skills provided for a smoothly run and effective program. Catherine Slight has been particularly helpful in preparing this manuscript for publication. We are grateful to our colleagues who provided leadership as facilitators or served as expert resource people: Dr. Christa Klein, Rev. James Walsh, Dr. Raymond Williams, Rev. Donald Senior, Rev. Thomas Esselman, Dr. Malcolm Warford, Dr. Jeanne McLean, Rev. Rufus Whitley, O.M.I., and Rev. Andrew Ciferni.

A final word of gratitude goes to the more than one hundred and fifty persons involved in theological education who participated in the Keystone Conferences. We hope that they find in these pages not only their own voice, but also the contribution they have made to building communities of wisdom both in theological education and in other areas of ministry in the Church.

Participating Institutions in the Keystone Conferences

Keystone Conference 1996

Saint John's Seminary, School of Theology, Brighton, Massachusetts
Saint John's Seminary, Camarillo, California
Saint John's School of Theology, Collegeville, Minnesota
Washington Theological Union, Washington, DC
Weston Jesuit School of Theology, Cambridge, Massachusetts

Keystone Conference 1997

Aquinas Institute of Theology, Saint Louis, Missouri
Catholic Theological Union, Chicago, Illinois
Mount Angel Seminary, St. Benedict, Oregon
Saint Mary's Seminary and University, Baltimore, Maryland
The Saint Paul Seminary School of Divinity, Saint Paul, Minnesota

Keystone Conference 1998

The Athenaeum of Ohio, Mt. St. Mary's Seminary, Cincinnati, Ohio
Oblate School of Theology, San Antonio, Texas
The Pontifical College Josephinum, Columbus, Ohio
Saint Meinrad School of Theology, St. Meinrad, Indiana
Seminary of the Immaculate Conception, Huntington, New York

Keystone Conference 1999

Jesuit School of Theology at Berkeley, Berkeley, California
Notre Dame Seminary, New Orleans, Louisiana
Sacred Heart School of Theology, Hales Corners, Wisconsin
Saint Vincent Seminary, Latrobe, Pennsylvania
University of St. Mary of the Lake, Mundelein Seminary,
    Mundelein, Illinois

Introduction

Imagine what the experience of the first Pentecost was like for both Jesus' disciples and the Jews "of every nation under heaven" who heard them. What preacher, teacher, or pastor wouldn't be envious? As the story is related in the Acts of the Apostles, the Jews who heard the disciples remarked:

> Are not all of these men who are speaking Galileans? How is it that each of us hears them in his native tongue? We are Parthians, Medes, and Elamites. We live in Mesopotamia, Judea and Cappodocia, Pontus, the province of Asia, Phrygia and Pamphylia, Egypt, and the regions of Libya around Cyrene. There are even visitors from Rome . . . Cretans and Arabs too. Yet each of us hears them speaking in his own tongue about the marvels God has accomplished (Acts 2:5-11).

Peter preached the Good News and three thousand were added to the community that day.

What a miraculous occurrence—to understand clearly what someone is saying who is not of one's culture and language. Imagine the astonishment of the preacher himself when he was understood and when three thousand people were moved to join the community.

Over two thousand years since that Pentecost experience, ministers of the church might long for something similar. How helpful it would be to repeat that ancient miracle in the Archdiocese of Los Angeles where the liturgy is celebrated in forty-two languages every Sunday; or in a seminary classroom where a teacher speaks to students whose first languages vary from English to Spanish, Vietnamese, Tagalog, and Arabic; or at a parish open forum where the principal languages of the parishioners are English, Spanish, Vietnamese, and French. In the United States today we might long for a similar "Pentecost" miracle that would prompt this kind of discourse: "Are not all of these ministers who are speaking North Americans? How is it that each of us hears them in our native tongue? We are Mexicans, Salvadorans, Guatemalans, Colombians, Peruvians, Filipinos, Vietnamese, Nigerians, Ghanaians, Russians, and Polish.[1] We live in the Southwest, New England, the Mid-Atlantic, the Plains States, the Pacific Northwest. Yet each of us hears them speaking in our own tongue." Would it not be wonderful to have the community of believers grow similarly in size and numbers today as in the days of the birth of the Church!

The idyllic community described in the early chapters of Acts almost immediately found itself facing new situations and pressures from outside and inside the community as it attempted to fulfill its mission to witness Christ to the ends of the earth. The members faced the Sanhedrin (Acts 5) and outright persecution from non-Christians, Saul being one of the most zealous (Acts 7:56, 8:1). From within the community questions arose as to those destined to hear the message. Peter eats with and preaches to Gentiles and stirs up the challenge as to whether the Good News should be preached to the Gentiles (Acts 11). The Hellenists complained that their widows were not being attended to properly, and new ministers arose to respond to the need (Acts 6). Each new challenge required adaptation on the part of the community so that they could continue the mission of Christ.

In ancient times and over the centuries, the community has made changes and adaptations that were consistent with the Good News and those that were not. The ongoing challenge is to remain faithful to the mission even as we experience the demands of a new age and new generations of believers.

The Christian community in the Catholic Church in the United States today finds itself again facing challenges as it attempts to continue its mission of testifying to Jesus Christ in the world and living as a community of witness. In an increasingly secular society, the Christian community must witness to a way of life that produces whole and holy people who testify to the truthfulness of the story of Jesus by their lives. Internally, church membership reflects nearly every race, language, culture, spirituality, and Christian theology in existence. While cause for great celebration, such differences do not always evoke a spirit of joy within the Christian community. Like our early predecessors in faith, we often get distracted by other issues and urgencies. We are always striving to live the wisdom reiterated by Pope John XXIII: "In essentials, unity, in doubtful matters, liberty, and in all things, charity."[2]

Three Challenges:
Diversity, Integration, and Assessment

This book focuses on three particular challenges for those who prepare people for the church's ministries and those working in ministry
itself: diversity, integration, and assessment. The essays examine what
each challenge means and they identify ways to respond that reflect the
deep marks of a theological vision through the lens of theological education. The material presented here draws on a six-year project called
the Keystone Conferences, funded by the Lilly Endowment and the
Bonfils-Stanton Trust administered by the Holy Name Province of
the Franciscan Friars. Entitled "Theological Teaching for the Church's
Ministries," the project involved twenty Catholic seminaries and
schools of theology in reflecting on the mission of their institutions
within the life of the Church as it becomes manifest in the processes of
teaching and learning.

Each summer, teams of six members from five different seminaries or
schools of theology spent a week in dialogue about what they were
learning about theological education and preparation for ministry in
the Church. Work in community was part of the project. Recognizing
the wealth of untapped wisdom in experienced educators, project
coordinators drew out the rich insights and knowledge within the
group with the assistance of facilitators. In so doing, participants
sharpened their focus on the essentials of their ministry as schools and
their need to adapt where necessary so that the institution's mission
could be realized. As these conversations continued over seven years,
the issues of diversity, integration, and assessment emerged as persistent and defining aspects of every school in some way.

These three issues touch the daily life of the entire Christian community, not just theological schools and seminaries. We hope that the
essays will be beneficial in appreciating the impact of diversity, integration, and assessment and in providing ways to respond to them in the
various communities where people gather to "devote themselves to
the apostles' teaching and fellowship, to the breaking of bread and the
prayers" (Acts 2:42).

Diversity

The challenge of diversity speaks to the reality in which the Church
exists and ministers. Gone are the days when the Catholic neighborhood

parish was the center of ecclesial and social life for families, where one ordinarily associated with "one's own," and where most were of one heart and mind. The current political, economic, social, and ecclesial reality reflects a pluralism that can be dazzling in its promise and overwhelming in its demands. How might we approach diversity in a way to tap its treasure while recognizing its limits?

Katarina Schuth's first chapter, "Diversity and the Formation for Ministry: Understanding the Challenge," identifies the sources of diversity in student populations in seminaries and schools of theology as historical, cultural, religious, educational, family background, age, and other factors. Her composite profiles of students representing these various diversities will call to mind current and former students or parishioners who make them real. Her essay is particularly helpful in looking deeper into the varieties of diversity that mark these people. Sister Schuth writes, "It is incumbent upon faculty members to study and analyze the backgrounds of those they teach in order to help maximize their educational experience and prepare more effective ministers." Those already involved in pastoral ministry and working with diverse groups of people will find connections to rapidly diversifying parish communities of faith and insights for more effective ministry.

Unfortunately, today's seminary professors or pastoral ministers do not know experientially the miracle of the first Pentecost. Their task is to teach and minister in a way that takes account of the diversity in student body and parish communities. How does one respond to the theological diversity among those whom one serves as well as to their unique requirements for learning? How are courses structured and classroom time organized? How does one preach or teach religious education to account for the breadth of backgrounds present in the congregation or classroom? Sister Schuth's second chapter, "Diversity and the Formation for Ministry: Principles and Practices," underscores the importance of establishing a hospitable environment where theological differences are respected and accepted and developing curricula and teaching methods are employed to meet wide-ranging learning needs. This same spirit of hospitality, she suggests, is the key to responsiveness to the diversity of parish life as well. She offers principles and practices gleaned from the Keystone Conferences as specific guides and strategies for teachers and pastoral ministers. At the heart of each principle and practice is the goal to tap into the treasure of diversity without allowing it to fragment individuals and the community itself.

Integration

If diversity is the challenge that characterizes the reality in which we live, integration is the goal toward which we strive. Integration is marked by wholeness, a balance within oneself and within a community. Its expression will be unique for different people and communities. Victor Klimoski provides a description of this goal in chapter 3, "Seeing Things Whole: A Reflection on Integration." Focusing primarily on the context of theological education, he defines integration as "a formative process that engages students in traditions of theological knowledge, pastoral practice, and Christian identity as they examine, re-interpret, and commit themselves to a worldview that bears the deep imprint of those traditions." So that integration is not a nebulous goal, faculties and parishes must be specific about what it should look like in students, parishioners, or parish communities (benchmarks), commit themselves to pursuing the goal (vision), and be quite specific as to how to get there (strategy). Dr. Klimoski offers concrete principles and practices for faculty and parish staffs as they minister in support of integration.

Assessment

Assessing progress along the journey toward integration is indispensable. Faculties often view the task of assessment as a pressure from outside the institution and therefore as an unwelcome intrusion into the life of the institution. In fact, assessment makes perfect sense. Who does not want to know if his or her energies are productive? How does one judge whether progress toward integration as an individual, faculty, or institution is being made without stepping back to evaluate one's work? How do we know that our assertions about the practices and disciplines of community life are accurate? In chapter 4, "Assessment and Good Teaching," Dr. Klimoski highlights the role of assessment in revitalizing an institution. He writes, "Done well, assessment can contribute to the vitality of an educational institution, enrich the communal character of faculty life, engage students at a new level of responsibility, and cultivate a partnership with the local church that fosters mutuality, not struggle for control." Assessment, then, becomes indispensable to institutions as they pay attention to the work of their communities.

Responding to Diversity, Integration, and Assessment

While it is important to name the challenges that bear in significant ways on the future of theological education, the Keystone Conferences explored how a faculty moves from *understanding* to *action*. Kevin O'Neil's chapter 5 focuses on building a community of wisdom energized for mission. The underlying assertion is that communities often enjoy considerable wisdom and energy for creatively responding to changing circumstances and needs that go untapped. In chapter 6, Father O'Neil describes specific processes that can be employed by communities in order to tap into the wisdom within them. It also addresses principles for the successful use of group processes.

The Environment for Our Work as Educators and Ministers

This book in part chronicles a significant intervention into the way Catholic theological schools and seminaries do their work. The Keystone Conferences provided a setting and context in which critical questions affecting the quality of that work might be examined with the fresh perspectives that emerge as colleagues from different schools and points of view search for insight and strategic ways to respond. In the last several chapters of the book, we invited colleagues to comment on issues that shape and define the environment in which the work of theological education occurs and toward which all its efforts are directed.

Because this book finds its focus in pedagogical practice, we wanted to address pedagogy from an angle that sharpened its task and reflected its complexity. We felt that looking at pedagogy through the lens of educational technology helped accent two realities. First, discussions of pedagogy ultimately return to the ability of teaching methods to facilitate learning. Second, the recent and most revolutionary pedagogical tool has been the Internet and other media used to stimulate learning. In chapter 7, Thomas Esselman, C.M., who is both an accomplished systematic theologian and a skilled classroom teacher, describes this new tool and its pedagogical implications. The ideas he poses and the questions he asks reflect renewed attention to the work of classroom teaching in theological education.

In chapter 8, Jeanne McLean and Donald Senior, C.P., draw on their years of experience in administration as they explore what it means to lead change processes in order to take institutional mission seriously. Focusing on the context and process for change, they argue that good leadership requires attention to the tension between mission and factors, whether internal or external, that support or resist change. Moreover, Dr. McLean and Father Senior reemphasize the need to cultivate broad ownership for new ideas and initiatives among constituents so that all share in their accomplishment.

The final chapter in our volume presents the reflections of six people who experience the work of the Church from different angles. Each responds to the issues raised in the book from their particular vantage point. Sr. Mary C. Boys, S.N.J.M., Ed.D., Skinner and McAlpin Professor of Practical Theology at Union Theological Seminary in New York, is an expert in religious education. Most Reverend Ricardo Ramirez, C.S.B., speaks as a pastoral leader of the Diocese of Las Cruces, New Mexico. Peter Steinfels, author and religion editor for the *New York Times*, draws on his broad knowledge of culture and religious engagement in American church life. Dr. Kathy Brown, a lay pastoral minister in Arlington, Virginia, and Fr. Barry Strong, O.S.F.S., pastor of Immaculate Conception Church in Wilmington, North Carolina, both consider the ideas and issues raised in this volume as leaders in parish communities. Finally, Raymond Williams, founding director of the Wabash Center for Teaching and Learning in Theology and Religion and professor emeritus in the department of religion at Wabash College, offers a commentary enriched by his extensive work across denominations with seminaries and departments of religion as they engage the same issues that captured the attention of those who participated in the Keystone Conferences.

Facilitating Ongoing Conversion

A common response to challenges that confront us is to point outside ourselves to others who need to change. In fact, however, the ongoing task for all of us is to be continually converted. The parable of the Prodigal Son (Luke 15) reminds us that conversion is about coming to "one's senses," or, more precisely, coming to oneself. Whether we are speaking of the challenge of diversity that we encounter within ourselves in the form of incompatible desires, thoughts, and feelings or the diversity within our parish communities or student bodies, our goal is to strive for wholeness. The chapters in this collection attest to the ongoing nature of this task. We never fully arrive this side of heaven. Yet it is a task worth pursuing. It is, ultimately, the journey of conversion. Thirty some years ago, Bernard Lonergan described conversion in this manner:

> Conversion is existential, intensely personal, utterly intimate. But it is not so private as to be solitary. It can happen to many, and they can form a community to sustain one another in their self-transformation and help one another in working out the implications and fulfilling the promise of their new life. Finally, what can become communal, can become historical.[3]

The Acts of the Apostles tells the story of the first Christians whose personal conversion led to the formation of a community and a Church that endures today. Our experience at the Keystone Conferences and in subsequent years is that the conversion of individual faculty members and faculties as a whole had historical consequences for academic institutions. We believe that ongoing efforts to meet the challenge of diversity by seeking integration aided by assessment will enhance theological education and form effective parish ministers and communities of faith. We do all that with great hope because the mission we have been given amazes us still.

NOTES

1. These groups represent the largest segments of legal immigrants into the United States from 1991–1996. See Bryan T. Froehle and Mary L. Gautier, *Catholicism U.S.A.: A Portrait of the Catholic Church in the United States*, Center for Applied Research in the Apostolate (Maryknoll, N.Y.: Orbis Books, 2000) 12.

2. John XXIII, *Ad Petri Cathedram* (1959) 72.

3. Bernard Lonergan, *Method in Theology* (New York: Herder and Herder, 1972; reprint ed., New York: The Seabury Library of Contemporary Theology, 1979) 130.

CHAPTER 1

Diversity and the Formation for Ministry: Understanding the Challenge

PART I: WHO ARE OUR MINISTRY STUDENTS? A PORTRAIT OF DIVERSITY

Introduction

Diversity, more than any other single characteristic, defines the student bodies of most seminaries and theologates at this time in history. The sources of diversity are multiple: cultural, religious, and educational, as well as place of origin, family background, personality, age, and life experience. The twenty theological faculties represented at the Keystone Conferences gave witness to the immediate impact of this reality on the life of the school, and its potential long-term impact on the life of the Church. As educators, they were in the process of adapting their teaching methods to meet the learning needs and ministerial expectations of individuals who no longer fit into the more homogeneous categories of a half-century ago.

Gone are the days when twenty-two to twenty-six-year-old men fresh from college seminaries and religious novitiates filled major seminaries. Coming from stable families of practicing Catholics, mostly of Irish, German, Italian, and Polish heritage, they shared a common experience of a dense Catholic culture, often lived out in a single parish with its own elementary and secondary school. As youth they served at Mass regularly and attended every Sunday, if not daily. These seminarians knew what the Catholic Church was about and what it meant to be a priest. Years of apprenticeship as an "assistant"—sometimes for as many as twenty-five years—were eventually rewarded with a pastorate. The young men who went through seminaries could anticipate a future that was predictable and contained.

1

In the twenty-first century the once routinized ministerial world has become dauntingly complex. So too has the work of major seminaries and theologates and what they need to do to equip students for pastoral leadership. Lay students join in classes and programs with seminarians in varying degrees and different proportions in each school. Each individual student has a unique profile, arising not only from dramatic cultural and ecclesial shifts since the 1960s, but also from wide-ranging life experiences. Seminarians will more quickly become pastors to serve large diverse parishes, or they will be pastors of two or more parishes. This changed situation prompts faculty to ask some challenging questions: What are the responsibilities of faculty, students, bishops, pastors, parishioners, and others to respond to diversity? Are there limits to the diversity any one school is capable of managing? In the midst of great diversity, what principles and practices can advance the way faculty members teach and learn for the sake of the church's ministries? If Catholics are to be served effectively in their parishes in the future, theological schools will need to continue their search for ways of responding to the issues raised here.

Part I describes the multiple sources of diversity by creating profiles of women and men who embody the personal and contextual influences that shape their character, personality, and spirit. Focusing on the varying learning styles and the differing ecclesiologies at work brings to the fore issues faculty face in teaching these students, both seminarians and lay. Creating these portraits keeps in clear focus that we are not dealing with a problem, but with people formed in a variety of ways and under a variety of circumstances. Our response is not to "fix them" but to create learning environments in which their gifts and their potential for significant service in the Church can be cultivated.

Part II investigates some of the sources of diversity highlighted in the profiles, including differences among students and within and between groups in light of their heritage, cultural experience, education, and religious ecclesial background.[1] Finally, the chapter examines ways in which faculties have attempted to adapt their teaching to accommodate contemporary circumstances and the backgrounds of students.

Profiles of Diversity

Each of these nine profiles portrays typical students enrolled in seminaries and theologates in this new century. Each profile relates information about family backgrounds and educational experiences before the time of theological studies for each student and then considers the particular issues faculty face in educating and forming these individuals.

Seminarians

Ronald. A consistent practitioner of his faith since childhood, Ronald, age twenty-five, is a second-year seminarian who enjoys the varied methods faculty employ in their teaching, especially when he is able to compare some of their theological positions to those he heard about in college seminary. His lifelong experience in an established and fairly affluent suburban parish gave him a confident sense of his faith, and he appreciated the involvement of many parishioners in ministries. Even now he is most at ease with liturgies like those he participated in a thousand times—lively contemporary music, lots of people taking liturgical roles, and generally meaningful homilies. He is also familiar with a few regular devotions—stations during Lent, rosary in May, and occasionally some special events like a parish mission. His parish was a comfortable place where everyone got along quite well. His family had lived in the community for three generations, and they enjoyed spending time at home and with neighbors. Vacations to visit his uncle up north, almost two hundred miles away, were far enough to travel as far as the whole family was concerned.

Ronald's college education began at a local Catholic university, but by his junior year he knew it was time to respond to a persistent call to priesthood. The college seminary helped him become more faithful to daily Mass and personal prayer, and he quickly found a group of seminarians with whom he had a great deal in common. His grades improved, and he developed good study habits. The most difficult episode during those last two years of seminary college was the required service-learning project that took him to an inner city school for two weeks to work with children newly arrived from Somalia. Ronald found it almost impossible to understand them. He really did not know what this experience had to do with seminary formation, but he toughed it out and didn't let his formation team know how he really felt. He didn't want to make too many waves.

Now in major seminary Ronald was finding his classes more than satisfactory, and he enjoyed the prayer life of the community and the camaraderie of his friends. His formation adviser raised some concerns, though, that bothered Ronald a lot. Father Ned pointed out Ronald's rather narrow approach to church and his need for broader experiences that would awaken him to the diversity of church membership. Father Ned had seldom noticed Ronald associating with any students from other countries, who were now a growing part of the seminary student body. The field placements he had chosen were generally in parishes much like the one he had known as a child, and he didn't care to volunteer for Sunday nights in the local soup kitchen. He had chosen not to participate in the summer program in Hispanic ministry and failed to see much point in visiting different ethnic parishes during his first-year Pastoral Ministry course. Ronald thought he could just keep a low profile, not complain too much, and then get ordained for the church he knew and loved. What could the faculty do about all this anyway? He was certainly going to be ordained, and he would make it clear to the bishop that his real skills were in serving the type of church community in which he had always participated.

Louis. When he was in his twenties, Louis had little time for his parents and siblings and even less for his faith. He was preoccupied with his business career and had made great progress toward earning enough money to buy a new house and just about any other luxury he wanted. His success, he felt, was the result of keeping focused and following company rules. Then one summer he was traveling to a business conference and found himself sitting next to a priest on the plane. It was a long flight so when the meal was served they began a conversation. Louis did not expect to be impressed, but the more Father Gene talked, the more Louis was taken with the quality of his life and the character of the people he worked with in his ministry. After that trip the thought of priesthood never left him.

At thirty-five Louis entered a pre-theology program and struggled some to keep up with his peers who had a much different educational background. Some of them had studied history and English and seemed to understand much more easily than he did the abstract ideas that were part of every philosophy course. Louis was diligent and soon began to comprehend the point of his studies. He just had to memorize a lot and not think too far beyond what was expected. Now at thirty-nine and in third theology, Louis had really had it with his teachers. What was wrong with learning one way to understand the faith and one way to do things? Recently, he wrote to his bishop about two of the faculty who were suggesting theological opinions Louis tried in vain to find in the *Catechism*. What more did he have to know than what he found there?

The faculty generally was getting on his nerves. The annual evaluation last year had not gone well because quite a few teachers noted Louis's seeming disinterest in broadening his horizons. They felt he was focused on getting through seminary without really being affected by the formation program. Louis simply did not understand the problem. What was wrong with just learning what was necessary without getting into these so-called theological opinions? After all, he wasn't going to teach theology; all that would be required was that he say Mass and preach. He was going to be a parish priest who would be good at managing the parish given his business background and sense of how an organization works.

Binh. It had been only four years since Binh left the internment camp in Cambodia heading for a midwestern seminary where at the age of thirty-two he began the pre-theology program. His life since then seemed like a roller coaster ride. He was welcomed to the seminary, but quickly learned that his English was quite inadequate for graduate studies. He spent the next two years trying to cram in courses in philosophy and theology with separate lessons in English. It was a struggle, especially with no family or old friends to support him. Though other students seemed cordial, he found it difficult to relate on more than a superficial level.

Gradually Binh settled into a routine of study and prayer, and several of his classmates helped him with schoolwork. Intent on following all the directives that were given, he wouldn't think of questioning or contradicting his teachers. Binh was more than shocked to hear how his new friends spoke up in class. He wondered how they dared interrupt with questions! When his first evaluation was presented to him, Binh was surprised about criticism of his silence in class. He thought he was being respectful.

Now after nearly four years in seminary, Binh was beginning to understand expectations for class participation, but he was still uncomfortable with the free exchange of ideas in discussion groups where there was no real authority figure monitoring what was being said. His last conversation with his formation adviser had been particularly troubling. He learned his English still wasn't good enough. Although he understood most of what people said, others had to ask him to repeat his comments. Some faculty were suggesting that Binh might benefit from a pastoral year. Such an idea spoke to him of failure. He left his adviser's office without giving him any hint of discouragement. He would never do that. Rather, he sought support in the local Vietnamese community, particularly from the parish deacon, himself a native of Vietnam, who was well acquainted with American customs after twenty years. Because Binh could discuss his real concerns with the deacon, he wouldn't have to worry as much about talking to his formation adviser.

James. When he was finishing high school, the guidance counselor suggested to James that he consider a technical school or maybe the community college for his education. Other colleges seemed out of reach, given the difficulty James had with his studies. Then something happened. At Mass one Sunday, Father Peter, the diocesan vocation director, gave a talk about the need for priests and he invited young men to consider the path toward ordination. James actually had thought of priesthood occasionally, but no one encouraged him much. In his public high school the topic wasn't even on the radar screen. In addition, his family went to Mass only occasionally, so they were certainly not thinking of the possibility. The first thing James did was to contact the vocation director, who was enthusiastic about having him start college seminary in the fall.

The first year was difficult. James failed a few courses and decided to drop out, but his vocation director encouraged him just to take a leave of absence and enroll for a semester or two at a community college. He tried for a year and he earned all Cs and even one B, so he was readmitted to the college seminary. Sister Theresa, a retired English teacher, worked diligently with him on his writing skills, and his reading was improving somewhat although he still found it difficult to retain information. Perhaps he was dyslexic, his faculty adviser speculated, but that didn't turn out to be the case. Now twenty-seven years old and in the second semester of the major seminary, James struggled to keep on top of his studies while he attended to all the other demands of priestly formation. He loved his pastoral ministry assignment and voluntarily spent extra time in the parish. Everyone gave him high marks for his participation in seminary life.

Then in his second year of theology things fell apart. James' classes were simply beyond him. He read the same pages over and over without comprehension. He tried studying with others, but they were not willing to spend lots of extra time with him, and their notes were even too much for James to grasp. His conviction about having a vocation never waivered. His formation advisor began asking James if he had ever considered another career. "That's a strange question," James thought, "coming from someone who was supposed to be encouraging me toward priesthood." His vocation director certainly wanted him to continue. Maybe the answer was another seminary where the studies were less demanding.

Roberto. Fifteen years ago, at age fourteen, Roberto's family had come from Mexico. He had enjoyed his high school experience and was very popular with other students, even though they teased him a little about his accent and his English grammar. He took it in stride and graduated without any problem. Even though he was not an academic star, Roberto went to a large state college where he earned a degree in computer science, making the most of his technical savvy. No one in college talked about his English fluency, and he knew he was getting better at it.

Roberto easily got a job after he graduated but was always a bit unsettled. Ever since he had participated in a Cursillo during his junior year, he felt a call to the priesthood but put it on hold until he finished college—secretly hoping the call would go away since his family was not likely to support his being a priest. After working for a few years, he had to talk to someone about the persistent call. Roberto sought out a religious priest at the college who had been welcoming when he was there. Father Raymond was enthusiastic and, after a few conversations over the next year, Roberto decided to enter the novitiate. All seemed to go well. After novitiate, Roberto began philosophy studies. The courses were tough, but with all kinds of help he passed.

When he entered theology, Roberto was anxious that the teachers were not from his own community. He was somewhat lost without his peers. Almost right away his Scripture professor told him his written exegesis papers, filled with grammatical errors, were unacceptable. Father Sylvester, his academic adviser, told him his spoken English would eventually be understood, but that he had to improve immensely before he could pass courses in theology. All these years Roberto had gotten by with help from his friends, but no one had addressed his basic problem with English. Fortunately, he had a good mind and was willing to do just about anything to continue in the priestly formation program. It might prove embarrassing, but Roberto even considered the suggestion that he take a year off from theological studies to focus on his English language skills.

Lay Students

Charlene. After almost ten years as a religious education coordinator, Charlene decided to upgrade her credentials in theology so she could qualify for a wider variety of pastoral positions. At the age of thirty-seven, she knew she wanted to have more flexibility in her ministry options. She noticed how many parishes in her home diocese had pastors responsible for two or three parishes, so more and more pastoral administrators were being hired. Such a position appealed to Charlene, who knew her background in religious education would be an asset in understanding overall parish operations. Her decision to enroll in the diocesan seminary was not easy since she would have to pay most of the tuition herself. The parish offered a small continuing education stipend, and the school gave a ten percent break on tuition. The cost in dollars and time was still significant.

It took some adjustment the first semester to get used to studies again and to fit them in with work and family. Gradually familiar habits of study returned, and the courses grew increasingly interesting. Charlene enjoyed participating in discussions, and the faculty appreciated the contributions she made based on her pastoral experience. She found, however, that seminarians were not as open to her comments. After some initial attempts at conversation with them during breaks, Charlene finally decided to seek out other lay students enrolled in the class with common interests and parish backgrounds. Charlene voiced her disappointment to several faculty members about the apparent lack of collaborative spirit among seminarians. She was more than a little surprised to learn that her quite assertive presence in class might be part of the reason for relational problems.

Charlene had more to learn than she had anticipated. In conversations with her faculty adviser, she began to explore some areas for her own professional development, such as how to organize staff meetings, deal with conflict, and deepen her theological understanding. These would serve her well in future leadership positions. She discovered that her attitude was changing in her present ministry, too, making it possible to strengthen relationships with the pastor, her staff peers, and volunteers. Finding just the right courses to continue her growth was a challenge since many faculty were focused more on theory than practice. Time and money continued to plague her progress, so she needed some assistance with both time management and finances. She also wanted to find a way to share more with seminarians since the future might well include one of them as her pastor.

Jonathan. Ever since he had participated in youth ministry programs, Jonathan wanted to work for the Church. When he was growing up, he enjoyed all the activities associated with the parish and participated in every activity he could. He appreciated the order and security he found in his parish, quite unlike the chaos of his family life. His parents both worked, leaving him and his three siblings as teenagers to fend for themselves. The family attended Mass fairly regularly, though not usually together. Jonathan knew that after finishing college he would try to find a position in some kind of church ministry. He began by serving in a medium-sized parish as a youth minister, but he assisted in lots of other ways as well. Jonathan appreciated the pastor who was very conscientious about how he said Mass and the way he preached. He never deviated from the rules.

After a few years, Jonathan decided to continue his studies so he could learn more about his faith and eventually be able to serve in other positions. Generally, he depended greatly on the pastor for knowing what to do and what to teach. Shortly after Jonathan enrolled in the Master of Arts in Pastoral Studies (MAPS) program at the local seminary, he felt his faith threatened. He had no idea there were such things as "theological opinions" or different ways to interpret Scripture. His sense was that all he had to do was memorize a lot of material. The class on Synoptics he was taking shook him to the foundations. He had never heard of historical-critical method much less seen it applied to the Bible. When he told his former pastor about what was happening, the pastor told him to just ignore all the theory. In fact, the pastor supplied him with one of his old textbooks so that he would not get too confused.

This tactic helped for a while, but when Jonathan talked to his faculty adviser, he let him know how upset he was by the content of the classes. It wasn't that the subject matter was too difficult. Jonathan simply disagreed with what was being taught. His adviser expressed concern about whether or not Jonathan could actually finish his degree, especially when he heard from several faculty members that he was becoming somewhat disruptive in class, frequently voicing his resolute opinions. As much as he seemed to like the practice of ministry, Jonathan was unable to apply what he was studying to what he most wanted to do.

Elizabeth. Even though Elizabeth was only twenty-three, she had decided early that she wanted to be a college theology professor. When she was completing her religious studies major with a 4.0 grade point average, members of the faculty encouraged her to apply for graduate school. After looking into several possibilities, Elizabeth thought her best bet was to enroll in the master's degree in the theologate close to her home. The convenience of the location was a major factor, and the theology professors were also excellent. She knew that the school was mainly for men from several religious communities who were studying to be priests, but that did not deter her.

During the first year, Elizabeth found the studies challenging but not beyond her grasp. Her relationships with other students were not as easy. Most of the other lay students were a little older, had some experience beyond college, and were usually married with children. The seminarians had their own communities and were not really looking for companionship either, so Elizabeth felt quite alone. She had always enjoyed studying with others, but few opportunities presented themselves. At times she really began to doubt her choice of schools, and even her vocation.

Before beginning her second year, Elizabeth explored with her adviser whether she should continue school or go out to work for a while. She had a hard time with reflection papers, and the pastoral dimensions of courses were perplexing. Recognizing that her ultimate goals were not directed toward ministry, she was trying to discern what the next best step should be.

Stephen. After completing his law degree, Stephen worked for several years at a small law firm whose work centered on public interest law—assuring access to justice for many people who were poor and marginalized. This work was frequently draining, both spiritually and emotionally. Thus, he felt that a deeper grounding in theology might help sustain him in his profession. He decided to return to school to get a master's degree in theology while continuing to work part time with a small caseload of clients. Because he had been working for a public interest firm, his salary was modest and he had little savings. This meant that his decision to return to school would involve a financial sacrifice.

Stephen grew excited about his studies, with a special fondness for moral theology and Scripture. He continued to study and work at an almost frantic pace in order to get everything accomplished. After a while he became a bit disillusioned with students who seemed less diligent about their studies and indifferent to the plight of the poor. He just couldn't understand how they could be so seemingly cavalier about something so important. Occasionally he found himself in heated conversations about the political-religious situation. Stephen began to wonder if he had found the right school.

These few profiles provide only a sample of the distinctiveness of students enrolled in seminaries and theologates. Students differ not only in what they bring to their studies, but also in the ministries in which they eventually will be functioning. The profiles might serve as the basis for a case study approach to the questions and concerns about students. With small adjustments, similar cases could be developed for other ministerial contexts. The case of Charlotte, for example, might be looked at from the perspective of the parish staff where she is presently serving. Her colleagues might help her by suggesting ways of approaching seminarians or topics she could raise in class that would have broad appeal to include seminarians. Profiles of the seminarians often reflect typical parishioners of the same age, introducing possible responses to the type of ministry that would be appropriate, for example, for recent immigrants or for persons whose command of English left them baffled during liturgy.

PART II: SOURCES OF STUDENT DIVERSITY

In the preceding section, the profiles of several prototypical students help to capture many of the qualities of those studying in seminaries and theologates. When faculty members at the Keystone Conferences discussed teaching and learning for the church's ministries, they noted how complex the task becomes when students with such varied backgrounds enroll in large numbers in a given school or dominate a particular course. Among the differences of greatest consequence were heritage, culture, education, and church experience (see Chart A). Information varies considerably for elements in each of these categories, ranging from detailed and precise data collected in surveys to observations of faculty and anecdotal reports of other observers, such as pastoral ministry supervisors, vocation directors, and parish staff members who work with students who are preparing for ministry.[2]

Chart A

Characteristics of Seminary and Theologate Students

Personal Sources of Diversity

HERITAGE

- family background, relationships
- racial, ethnic background
- personality, character
- religious background
- age, health

EDUCATION

- natural intellectual abilities
- openness to learning
- educational background
- learning experiences
- learning style preferences
- learning problems

CULTURE

- place of origin
- language background
- cultural experience
- intercultural experience
- attitude toward culture
- socio-economic class

CHURCH

- theological/religious position
- liturgical preferences, worship experiences
- spiritual experiences, spirituality
- devotional life
- ministerial images/goals

Heritage

The heritage of those entering church ministry includes such basic information about students as family backgrounds and relationships, racial/ethnic profiles, personality and character, religious backgrounds, and age and health. The most precise and comprehensive information is available on racial/ethnic backgrounds and ages of ministry candidates. Even though it is to a lesser extent, we also know from faculties and other observers a good deal about students' families of origin, their personality, character, and overall well-being. Much is known about their religious backgrounds.

Racial/Ethnic Backgrounds. Of the 3,065 seminarians enrolled in major seminaries in 2003–2004, white Anglo students comprised 66 percent, while 14 percent were Hispanic/Latino, 12 percent Asian, 5 percent Black, and 3 percent other.[3] Within these categories, subsets generate

Table 1: Race/Ethnicity 2003–2004

Race/Ethnicity	Seminarians	Lay Students (all)	Faculty
White Anglo	66%	71%	92.3%
Hispanic/Latino/a	14%	22%	4.6%
Asian	12%	2%	1.6%
Black	5%	3%	1.2%
Other	3%	2%	0.3%
	100%	100%	100%

even more diversity, for example, Hispanic/Latino encompasses Mexican, Puerto Rican, Colombian, and Dominican, and many others. The length of time seminarians have spent in the U.S. and the nature of their interaction with American communities add further distinctions. American-born students from these racial/ethnic groups who still possess a strong sense of their origins also contribute to the variety.

Describing the profile of lay students studying in seminaries and theologates is not so simple since the only comprehensive data available also include those preparing for lay ecclesial ministry in programs sponsored by local dioceses. The Center for Applied Research in the Apostolate (CARA) statistics show that 25,964 women and men were enrolled in ministry formation programs in all settings in 2003–2004. Approximately ten percent of them were studying with priesthood candidates in seminaries and theologates.

The racial/ethnic composition of all lay students was 71 percent white Anglo, 22 percent Hispanic/Latino/a, three percent Black, two percent Asian, and two percent other (see Table 1). Informal polling suggests that those studying in seminaries and theologates are more likely to be white Anglo and less likely to be Hispanic/Latino/a than the full complement of lay students.

Of great importance in these numbers is the fact that one-third of seminarians and just over one-fourth of lay students are from racial/ethnic backgrounds other than the vast majority of those who have been traditional members of the church in the U.S. They are different as well from most faculty, of whom only 7.7 percent are other than white Anglo.[4] Another factor is the rapidity of change in the racial/ethnic composition of students during the past ten to fifteen years: in the early

1990s only about ten percent of students were from minority groups. Most faculty are of an age where they neither studied with minority students nor ministered in parishes with large minority populations. Thus, the backgrounds of many faculty are remarkably different from these present-day students, and their experience with racial/ethnic minorities is quite limited.

Age. Seminarians on the whole are much younger than lay ecclesial ministry students. In 2003-2004, nearly half of the seminarians were between the ages of twenty-five and thirty-four and another 15 percent younger than twenty-five, while 16 percent were thirty-five to thirty-nine, and 20 percent were over forty. Of all lay students, only nine percent were under thirty, compared to 42 percent of seminarians; 17 percent were from thirty to thirty-nine, compared to 38 percent of seminarians; 32 percent were from forty to forty-nine, compared to 13 percent of seminarians; and 42 percent were over fifty, compared to seven percent of seminarians (see Table 2). While *degree-seeking* lay students enrolled in seminaries and theologates are younger than *all* lay students, they are still significantly older on average than seminarians.

What difference does age make in theological schools? The dominant, but not the only, apprehension arises because of differences between the ages of most students and faculty. The average age of faculty is fifty-four, while the average age of students is about twenty years younger. One faculty member lamented that current students are looking for role models different from what older faculty are able to provide. The expectations of Generation X and Generation Y are neither obvious nor clearly understood by the older generation. The battles fought by faculty are not necessarily the battles students care to engage. For example, generational differences may come to light when faculty present the complexity that is part of the Catholic faith experience while students are seeking certainty about theological issues. Younger students who have not experienced the well-structured educational background their teachers had prize simplicity and clarity. Their questions are more likely to focus on whether or not they will find faith: "Is there anything out there?" In part, this fear helps explain why "identity" markers associated with dress and devotional life loom so large. Given these differences, faculty need to be aware of their own built-in limitations when it comes to teaching and mentoring current students. To fully engage them, faculty members need to do their best to comprehend the mindset of the younger generations.

Table 2: Age 2003–2004

Age	Seminarians	Lay Ecclesial Students (all)
< 30	42%	9%
30–39	38%	17%
40–49	13%	32%
> 50	7%	42%
	100%	100%

As Table 2 illustrates, vast age differences are found **among students,** a reality creating some advantages as well as generating some difficulties for teaching and learning. The adage that suggests older students do not change as readily as their younger counterparts proves true in many cases, but faculty observe that it is sometimes the younger students who find change most problematic when it comes to their grasp of present-day church ministry. Generational differences regarding conflicting ideas about the nature of priestly identity are pervasive, too. This divide is key for the formation of new priests who will be working with older pastors. These differences show up, for example, in liturgical styles and devotional practices, such as the rosary and benediction or in the use of inclusive language. One faculty member noted that translations receiving the approval of the United States Conference of Catholic Bishops (USCCB) are not even good enough for some students. If the Pope has not agreed to the changes, they are considered invalid. Lest the differences between generations be exaggerated, it is important to note that many students are open and eager to learn. The question for faculty is why some students are unwilling to consider new approaches or interpretations about virtually any aspect of their faith.

Background: Family, Personality, and Character. Seminarians and lay students each present a somewhat different profile when considering how their backgrounds contribute to their receptiveness to formation for ministry. Most seminarians enter theological studies physically and psychologically healthy, with sufficiently outgoing personalities to conduct the public ministry required of the church's ordained. Faculty describe many of them as earnest, pious, and committed. They enter consciously into a formation process that asks them to accept criticism and to change their behavior and attitudes in conformity with the expectations of priesthood. Ministry today demands extensive collaboration, including skills in leading groups, running meetings, managing and delegating, and resolving conflicts. Those with a more extroverted personality tend to succeed in these roles more readily, and many seminarians can learn to respond to these demands. A significant minority is extremely introverted and passive by nature, and they are likely to find public ministry burdensome and demanding. The task of the seminary, in collaboration with others who supervise seminarians, is to determine whether or not each individual is capable of assuming the responsibilities of priestly ministry.

More comprehensive information about family backgrounds of the newly ordained can be garnered from *The First Five Years of the Priesthood.*[5] By extrapolating from the Hoge data, one can assume similar traits for current seminarians. Through surveys of newly ordained priests, Hoge found that

- A remarkable number of priests are sons of alcoholic fathers, and mothers who were dominant in their lives.

- Some priests experienced strong parental pressure for them to enter the priesthood.

- During adolescence, some priests were socially shy and did not participate in activities and relationships typical of their peer group.[6]

Clearly not all seminarians carry these traits, but when they do their attitude toward the seminary and future ministry is deeply affected. Some may experience resistance to formation, others lack internal commitment, and still others may find it difficult to embrace the relatively outgoing activities required in ministry.

Similar detailed information is not available about lay students, so it is necessary to rely mainly on anecdotal reports from faculty who work with these women and men in seminaries and theologates. Earlier in the chapter, we noted that lay students are somewhat older and are less diverse in terms of racial and ethnic backgrounds. Many of them are already working in parishes and other ministries, often married with families, and settled in their local parishes. Their choice to serve in full time ministry usually comes from a deep personal commitment to the Church. Since salaries are usually lower than comparable secular positions, their motivation is quite strong. Many of them struggle to balance multiple responsibilities while studying—family, work, and school—so they experience considerable stress and are usually able to study only part time.

Socio-cultural Background

In some ways, cultural factors can also be considered part of the heritage of students, but the complexity and importance of this dimension of diversity in the Church requires separate treatment. Seminarians and lay ecclesial ministry students come from considerably different cultural backgrounds, with the experience of seminarians much more varied. In 2003–2004, nearly one-fourth of seminarians came from other countries, and among those who are American citizens at least an additional fifteen percent are from U.S. minority groups. Besides place of origin, students differ in the extent of exposure they have had to other cultures in the U.S. and beyond its borders. This exposure, or lack of it, often determines the degree of openness students exhibit toward those from cultures other than their own.

Places of Origin and Cultural Background. Of particular interest is demographic information about where ministry students were born and grew to adulthood. In 2003–2004, some 744 seminarians, 23.7 percent, came from eighty-four countries outside the United States, and 85 percent of that group intend to stay here when they are ordained.[7] Unlike seminarians, virtually all lay ministry students are from the U.S. and intend to remain here to practice ministry. Their limitations come more from lack of opportunity to experience intercultural situations rather than from their lack of knowledge of U.S. culture.

The diversity characterized by these data gives an indication of the demands on educators and also suggests enormous challenges for parishes as newly ordained priests of varying cultural backgrounds are assigned to them. The task for lay ministers may be to help acculturate international priests for whom seminary is the only experience in this country before ordination. In most cases, those whose second language is English struggle with their academic courses as well as with pastoral understanding. Yet these students can be especially gifted in multicultural settings because of their familiarity with a culture other than the dominant culture.

Socio-economic Status. Though a clear depiction of the socio-economic status of students is not available, we can make a number of generalizations based on the observations of faculty and data from other sources dealing with cultural trends. Surveys show a decline over the past twenty years or so in the perceived status of clergy. During the same time, whether or not there is a correlation, seminarians are less likely to come from families where parents are professionals and more likely to come from middle-class families. In part this trend is related to the upward mobility of Roman Catholics in recent years and to the availability of college education for families from a wider income range.

Socio-economic status is difficult to compare or measure when looking at students coming from other countries. Invariably international students are less well off in a material sense, but often they have had the advantage of education beyond what their socio-economic status would indicate. They frequently have been educated in minor seminaries in their countries of origin and have completed a rather rigorous classical education. Yet their exposure to other cultures probably has been limited. The sudden transition to an American school is often fraught with difficulties when, for example, they are asked to participate in class discussions and write papers that require interpretation.

Lay ministry students tend to be from the middle class. When they are working for a degree in theology, finances are often an issue. For the majority, the pace of their education is necessarily slowed by their need to continue working and by family obligations. This adds a unique dimension to academic life since many lay students experience disruptions in their daily lives that interfere with their capacity to finish assignments and focus on their studies. Many are remarkable in their ability to transcend the difficulties of multiple responsibilities. Enrolling in cohort programs, where the schedule and pace are prescribed, provides many lay students with a built-in support system.

Education and Intellectual Aptitude

Though much has been said about educational levels of students, few current statistical studies are available. In research on theological education, faculty members clearly identify several categories of seminarians—though they are less specific about lay students—relative to their native intellectual abilities. Three levels of intellectual qualifications of seminarians are proposed: (a) those highly qualified, estimated to be about ten percent of all seminarians and thought to be a smaller proportion now than in the past; (b) mid-range students, making up over fifty percent, who have good capability for doing graduate theological work; and (c) students who experience one or more learning difficulties, who constitute the remaining *forty percent*. This last group creates special challenges for faculty who need to familiarize themselves with the learning problems faced by these students.

Natural Intellectual Abilities and Educational Backgrounds. The smallest group of ministry students, about ten percent of the whole, have had the advantage of a first-rate classical education, during which they studied philosophy along with some Scripture and theology. They understand the relationship between learning and the capacity to minister and can readily apply their learning to ministerial settings. Among these students are potential candidates for advanced theological study, which would prepare them to be future seminary faculty members or to serve in other leadership positions. Since they constitute a relatively small proportion of students in most seminaries, they may be overlooked or not adequately challenged because of the more basic needs of the majority of students.

Over half of all seminarians have reasonably good quality college degrees, adequate intellectual abilities, and openness to learning what the church teaches. They are challenged to integrate all aspects of their formation, which inspires many of them to spend hours in study, prayer, and pastoral placements. Many enter seminary with degrees in business, science, or technology, with less exposure to the humanities than in the past. This deficit in their backgrounds affects their study of theology and sometimes their ability to preach and engage in other forms of ministry that benefit from a liberal arts education. Careful analysis of the specific lacunae is important if these students are to reach their full potential.

The third group of just over one-third of students includes those who are less qualified for one of several reasons: some have weak educational backgrounds, others come with learning disabilities, and some are older students far-removed from formal education who sometimes find the return to studies problematic. Overall, approximately ten percent fall into each category, but sometimes seminaries will have a larger proportion of one or another of this type of student. In this third group are the twenty percent of international seminarians who may lack English language facility. Though many of these students are intellectually above average, they have difficulty with their academic programs because of insufficient knowledge of English. Sometimes the problem extends to pastoral practice because of lack of experience with American culture. Obviously, they need extensive support if they are to become adequate ministers of Word and Sacrament. Few faculty have been fully prepared to work with these students.

Openness to Learning and Learning Style Preferences. Regardless of native abilities and educational experiences, student attitudes about learning vary significantly and are vitally important to how well they engage the program. Their openness to learning has more effect on their ability to learn than do many other factors. Repeatedly, Keystone faculty participants lamented the unwillingness of some students to engage in the learning enterprise because of preconceived ideas about theology they did not wish to change. Typically these students prefer lectures based solely on church documents and presented without theological interpretations or opinions. Students who are older or who have had more ministerial experience tend to favor class discussions and a broader range of resources. In recent years many faculty have found the use of technology an essential tool that can help them vastly expand the resources available to students.

Ecclesial Outlook

A major divide between pre- and post-Vatican II priests is now well documented in *The First Five Years of Priesthood: A Study of Newly Ordained Catholic Priests*[8] and *Evolving Visions of Priesthood.*[9] This division is evident to faculty in seminaries and theologates, who—with the exception of a growing number of younger faculty—find themselves radically different from many of the students they teach. In the first of Hoge's studies, he describes seminarians as "firm in their loyalty to Pope John Paul II, their adherence to all church teachings about sexual morality and contraception, and their preference for tradition and formality in ritual and priestly roles."[10] The first study also shows that polarization, which is more acute than twenty years ago, extends beyond the seminary to the priesthood. The second study reaffirms the differences between older and newer priests and indicates that the self-identity of newer priests correlates with the cultic model of priesthood in contrast to the servant-leader model. These differences in perception about priesthood originate in the theological understandings that seminarians bring to their studies, as well as in their particular experiences of church and the stage of their faith journeys. They fear loss of the uniqueness of priestly ministry vis-à-vis lay ministry. The theological/ religious positions of lay students, who have their own characteristics, require special consideration in teaching as well.

Theological/Religious Backgrounds. Three broad categories encompass the religious backgrounds of most seminarians. We are beginning to see these categories among lay students as well. Some are deeply rooted in their faith, others are recently converted, and a smaller group enters seminary after only minimal connection to the church. In each of these groups, some distinctions can be made. For example, some may be oriented toward Vatican II teachings and favor further transformation of church practices along those lines, and others may seek restoration of some traditional practices. A few may comprise a fourth group whose stance toward church and life in general is rigid and unchanging even in the face of new information and evolving situations.[11]

THOSE DEEPLY ROOTED IN THEIR FAITH. Typically these individuals grew up in families where they practiced their faith consistently in a local parish and were involved beyond attendance at Sunday Mass. They have a moderately good grasp of the Catholic tradition, some sense of the church as universal, adequate religious education, and a long-standing commitment to their faith. About one-third of all people in this group have a realistic understanding of what their commitment to parish life will entail. Initially they approach their studies and ministry in a manner similar to what they experienced in the past. Those coming from a more traditional parish or college setting are likely to prefer something comparable. Others may be more likely to be comfortable with variety and adaptation. Since a high proportion of seminarians, especially those headed for diocesan priesthood, have experienced more traditional parish life, they tend to prefer what they know. However, a notable difference between seminarians in this group and those described below is their sense of confidence about their faith. Since they have grown up with considerable understanding of the church, they are usually not as threatened by diversity and new ideas, and thus more often they exhibit openness to learning.

THOSE RECENTLY CONVERTED. Two types of conversion experience typify this group of seminarians: those converted from another Christian denomination or, more typically, those baptized Catholics at birth but who have been away from the church for a number of years. Often those who are reconverted became aware of their vocational call through a significant religious experience—for example, during a pilgrimage to Medjugorje or at a large religious gathering. Sometimes they were deeply influenced by a charismatic person's commitment and dedication, typically a priest, who may have asked them if they had ever considered priesthood. These men usually have enjoyed only a short-term or sporadic association with a parish and thus lack familiarity with church teaching and life because of the rather sudden shift in their life direction.

A large number of seminarians, at least one-third, comes to theological studies as reconverted Catholics. One might expect that their personal change and transition would enhance their flexibility, but instead it often leads to a desire for security and stability in their newfound faith. Their relative lack of religious background and knowledge of the church's history can make them feel afraid of disturbing their minimal knowledge and of losing the security they have gained through their conversion. This attitude leads to a desire to have all formation conform exactly to their narrow experience. They may find difficulty in adapting their set notions about religious education, liturgical life, and other dimensions of ministry. The task for faculty is to introduce these students to the breadth of the Catholic experience and provide careful mentoring and supervision.

THOSE WITH A MINIMAL CONNECTION TO THE CHURCH. The seminarians in this category formally identify themselves as Catholic, but many have not practiced their faith consistently. Usually they have not attended Catholic schools and are experiencing formal religious education for the first time in seminary. They tend to fall into one of two groups: some are caught up by the Spirit and enter fully into the formation process, later becoming convincing models in parishes for people who themselves may have experienced what it is like to be indifferent to their faith; others never quite find their way and are apt to leave the seminary before ordination or, if ordained, fail to engage fully in parish ministry.

Those in the group who remain in the formation program through ordination, comprising about one-fourth of all seminarians, often are open to new information about their faith and are enthusiastic about ministry. Their engagement in class is inspired by their eagerness to serve parishioners who are struggling with the meaning of faith in their own lives. The lack of fervor of those whose commitment is tenuous makes it difficult for them to complete assignments or take formation seriously.

This group and the group who have recently experienced some type of conversion make up nearly sixty percent of all seminarians, according to faculty estimates. These estimates correlate well with the data in *The First Five Years of the Priesthood*, where nearly three-fourths of the recently ordained respondents reported that they experienced a spiritual awakening, something akin to a conversion, prior to entering the seminary. Thus, their limited familiarity with the church poses serious pedagogical problems for faculty.

THOSE WHO HAVE A RIGID UNDERSTANDING OF THEIR FAITH. Most often seminarians in this category, comprising less than ten percent of the total, came of age after Vatican II concluded and have no memory of the church before 1970. They have lived their entire adult lives to date during one single pontificate, a factor that helps explain their unswerving devotion to the present Pope and his writings, often to the exclusion of earlier church leaders and documents. While they have been greatly affected by American cultural forms like their peers, including media, technology, and communications, unlike their peers, their response is to withdraw and condemn the world as they see it. They tend to experience enormous fear—fear of change and fear of the world—and they regard seminaries as the last bastions of security.

This fourth group may overlap with any of the previous three groups and may well constitute the greatest challenge for faculty. Administrators and faculty describe this fourth type of student quite vividly. External signs may include an unhappy appearance, downcast eyes, tight body, and no sense of humor. Generally, these students express dissatisfaction with the seminary and criticize it for lacking sufficient devotion or orthodoxy, a stance often resulting from their own inadequate experience of the church. Without a broader perspective, they think of themselves as invariably right in their views about the church. The attitude of these students toward learning is that any new insight is a threat, and so they expect faculty to conform to their own thinking rather than introduce new insights. Such people tend to see things through a single lens, accepting only clear, distinct ideas that are aligned with their view of orthodoxy. They are not interested in discussion or dialogue and see the world only from their own perspective. As a result, they are drawn to defensive and fundamentalistic positions. These students tend to grasp at easily memorized formulas because they fear sophisticated and nuanced thinking; as a result they become suspicious of speculative thought simply because they cannot enter into it.

Factors such as varied ethnic and cultural backgrounds, countries of origin, first language other than English, age, and educational backgrounds complicate this picture even more. Liturgical preferences, spiritual experiences, devotional life, and spirituality are all affected by the personal qualities of these students. In almost every seminary, faculty puzzle over how to work with students' penchant for a plethora of devotions that limits their time for common liturgical celebrations. They want to encourage them to adapt their ministerial images and goals to the church that awaits them. The challenge for seminaries, and later for parishes, is to integrate these men first into American culture and then to parish life and other ministries that are equally diverse.

LAY STUDENTS. While one might expect lay students, who generally come from similar backgrounds, to have a comparable religious profile, the reality is in fact strikingly different. One of the major differences is that most lay ecclesial students have had at least some ministerial experience before their graduate theological studies. They are on the whole older than seminarians and have had more life experience in general. Because most of them are paying for their courses themselves, they strive to gain as much as they can from the faculty and are often able to use what they learn rather immediately. Though few have the background in philosophy of most seminarians, faculty report that their experience with church ministry more than suffices for the difference. Many of these students work in parishes where collaboration is expected and where Vatican II teachings prevail. Faculty members often report that they frequently find lay students more open to learning and more aware of the variety of situations they will face in ministry because of their exposure to the needs of parishioners.

Summary

Reviewing the heritage, socio-cultural backgrounds, education and intellectual aptitude, and experience of church of current lay and ordained candidates for ministry provides insight into the importance of approaching the teaching and learning process with care and reflection. Each student will receive the subject matter of theological education differently, so it is incumbent upon faculty members to study and analyze the backgrounds of those they teach in order to help maximize their educational experience and prepare more effective ministers. The "principles and practices" identified in the next chapter respond to the challenges faculty meet in contemporary ministry students.

NOTES

1. For a detailed description of seminarians, see Katarina Schuth, *Seminaries, Theologates, and the Future of Church Ministry* (Collegeville: Liturgical Press, 1999) 66–94.

2. Among other sources are data from several CARA studies and Dean Hoge's extensive work, specifically noted below.

3. All data in this section are from "Catholic Ministry Formation Enrollments: Statistical Overview for 2003–2004" (Washington, D.C.: Center for Applied Research in the Apostolate, 2004).

4. Data on seminary and theologate faculty are from the Auburn Center for the Study of Theological Education (2004). Further analysis shows a slight improvement among younger faculty in the proportion of racial/ethnic diversity: those 54 and under are 10.5 percent non-white and those over 54 are 4.7 percent non-white.

5. Dean R. Hoge, *The First Five Years of Priesthood: A Study of Newly Ordained Catholic Priests* (Collegeville: Liturgical Press, 2002); see especially ch. 2, "Attitudes of the Newly Ordained Active and Resigned Priests," 9–34.

6. Ibid., 83–86.

7. "Catholic Ministry Formation Enrollments: Statistical Overview for 2003–2004 (CARA)."

8. Hoge, *The First Five Years of Priesthood.*

9. Dean R. Hoge and Jacqueline E. Wenger, *Evolving Visions of the Priesthood: Changes from Vatican II to the Turn of the New Century* (Collegeville: Liturgical Press, 2003).

10. Hoge, 4.

11. Schuth, *Seminaries, Theologates, and the Future of Church Ministry,* 74–79. The text that follows is adapted from the research presented on the pages indicated.

CHAPTER 2

Diversity and the Formation for Ministry:
Principles and Practices

The wide range of diversity among ministry students requires approaches to teaching and learning that prepare all students for effective service. Three major tasks confront faculties: determining how to work productively with diverse student bodies; becoming more attuned to the ministerial requirements of the future; and initiating and expanding faculty development programs to assist them in responding to contemporary students. During the Keystone Conferences, participants identified principles and practices that would support their efforts in preparing ministers capable of working for the whole church. This work by participants represents a concrete response to how we might teach more effectively so that all students, like those profiled in the previous chapter, might learn. What these faculties have learned can also be useful to pastoral leaders who are experiencing the same range of diversities among parishioners.

Working Effectively in Contexts
with Diverse Student Bodies

The two sources of diversity requiring most attention are those related to different theological perspectives and changing requirements for effective learning. The practical experience of Keystone participants centered on two broad themes: creating a hospitable environment and developing a suitable formation program. Several principles and many practices give substance to these concepts.

Create a Hospitable Environment

PRINCIPLE 1. *Recognize that the meaning of Catholic identity is a major issue for students.*

Generational differences are key to understanding expressed student concerns about Catholic identity. Immersion in Catholic culture has been significantly deeper for persons over forty or fifty years of age, contrasted with the vast majority of seminarians and lay students who lack a solid sense of what it means to be Catholic. Few have had extensive experience with the church, and even fewer have benefited from in-depth religious education beyond elementary school. Thus they are more likely to be threatened by an education that reveals the complexity of church life.

Since the majority of faculty members are over age fifty, their secure sense of Catholic identity developed during a period of great change, which can be comforting to some students who may be threatened by any challenge to their own sense of the tradition. Faculty can explain how they managed to adapt and adjust to major shifts occurring after the Second Vatican Council. Even though students may experience the notion of a dynamic church as disconcerting, faculty can demonstrate the continuity of faith in the midst of external change. More importantly, they can help future ministers consider that their roles will certainly require openness to change.

PRACTICES:

Appreciating limitations:

- Recognize that Catholic identity was indeed more secure for people before Vatican II than for most students in the present generation.

- Understand that students with limited backgrounds in church life have a need to grow in and experience what it means to have an internalized identity as a Roman Catholic.

- Provide students with a way to interpret the complexity in their search for Catholic identity by discussing divergent opinions that exist within the tradition.

Identifying growth:

- Share examples of what the search for identity can lead to—positive and negative.

- Discuss with students what model of priesthood or ministry is most suitable for specific contexts.

- Help students cope with theological complexity by listening respectfully to them.

- Develop attitudes of patience and tolerance by encouraging students to converse outside of class about questions they have.

PRINCIPLE 2. *Establish and maintain an atmosphere of safety and trust in which all persons respect each other's opinions throughout the institution, especially in the classroom.*

This principle is critical, for without trust students find it difficult to learn, much less to engage in open dialogue. Ensuring a safe environment begins with orientation and continues through many encounters both inside and outside the classroom. On an institutional level, students must be encouraged to speak their mind on any issue as long as they do so with respect for all. They should be assured that they will not be dismissed because of the opinions they express, nor should they fear raising any issue that is important to them. When students articulate what they are feeling and thinking, no one should be permitted to disparage their opinion, though students should expect to be challenged by faculty and other students who disagree with them.

In the classroom, an appropriate confidentiality needs to be observed. This means that no one repeats the details of class conversations or names the persons involved and what they said. Faculty members can serve as models in sharing life experiences, including their own intellectual struggle with particular teachings of the church, and how they have dealt with them. By using the pronoun "I," students grow accustomed to owning their opinions and viewpoints and taking responsibility for explaining why they arrive at their conclusions.

In formal classroom settings students may feel intimidated for various reasons: a natural shyness or reluctance to speak in groups, cultural values that include excessive deference toward a teacher, or worry about being dismissed from the program because of stating a controversial opinion. Certain techniques can overcome concerns about shyness and deference, such as asking all students to speak briefly in turn or having them reflect and write notes before requesting an oral response from them.

Some practices that increase trust and confidence take place outside the classroom. If students express strongly conflicting views that cannot be settled during class, they should be encouraged, perhaps with the faculty member's presence, to continue the discussion privately at a later time. Also, faculty might recommend to students that they discuss some matters of conscience with a spiritual director or other personal issues with a formation adviser. In any case, students should understand that what they articulate in honest and respectful intellectual discourse will not result in a negative evaluation.

PRACTICES:

Facilitating participation:

- Actively encourage students to voice their opinions respectfully and then carefully listen to them.

- Never disparage a student's opinion or allow disparagement by other students.

- Put the best construction on each contribution to class discussion, perhaps by way of adding to a point being made, asking a question, or, after trust is established, disagreeing in a constructive way.

- Let students know they will not be dismissed from the program because of opinions they articulate.

- Refrain from making negative judgments about the intent of the insights students share or ascribing unfair motives to them.

- State explicitly how the principle of confidentiality in the classroom will operate.

Modeling openness:

- Share appropriate life experiences and acknowledge one's own struggles in coming to understand and embrace church teachings.

- Show students that you are willing to learn by acknowledging new insights you gain from their contributions.

- Personalize dialogue by using students' names and model taking responsibility for one's own ideas by using the pronoun "I."

- Create an institutional culture that allows real and sometimes controversial issues to surface for discussion.

Integrating formation:

- Deal with inappropriately heated expressions of disrespect or defiance in a one-to-one conversation outside the classroom as soon as possible.

- Encourage students to bring unresolved issues to appropriate persons outside the classroom, such as a formation adviser or spiritual director.

- Make sure the evaluation process does not compromise the "safe" atmosphere in the classroom.

PRINCIPLE 3. *Make diversity acceptable.*

Theological educators need to become acquainted with the composition of their particular student bodies and then, in their teaching, take into account the distinctiveness of students. Raising awareness about differences in cultural backgrounds, age, and experience not only in the class, but also in the church generally, is an essential step in dealing successfully with diversity. Faculty should alert students to the variety of backgrounds represented by their peers and demonstrate how exposure to differences can enhance their future ministry. Students should be asked to share aspects of their religious history and articulate how their experiences have led to their distinctive expressions of faith.

Especially in the initial years of the students' formation, faculty members should establish an environment where all are welcome and where different viewpoints can be voiced. The value of diversity cannot be underestimated, and its contribution to learning should be actively acknowledged. Solicit examples of practices that emphasize the strengths of various cultures, such as strong family values, a contemplative stance toward life, or energetic liturgies. As students grow in appreciation for the richness of various cultural expressions of the faith, they are more likely to incorporate them in their own ministry.

Certain teaching techniques are beneficial in promoting acceptance. By assigning tasks to various participants in discussions, by giving special encouragement to shy or reluctant students, and by restating comments in a more understandable way, teachers can expand the range of experiences introduced in the classroom. From time to time, through creative evaluative practices, faculty should discern how well and what students are learning, where problems exist, and how to overcome difficulties.

PRACTICES:

Understanding variation:

- Analyze the makeup of the student body so that teaching and learning can be adapted to its particular characteristics.

- Acknowledge differences in age, background, and experience of students in each class by helping students develop a profile of who they are, what they have done, and what they know/think about the topic of the course.

- Emphasize how theological learning can be enhanced because of diverse cultural, educational, and religious backgrounds.

Setting the tone:

- Establish an environment of tolerance, inclusion, and acceptance where all theological understandings are open for discussion and review.

- Model an approach to theology that incorporates a variety of viewpoints and includes ongoing dialogue.

- Let students know that diverse views are respected by showing appreciation for the varied ways theological positions can be expressed.

Identifying and valuing diversity:

- Evoke from students their own experiences of how they learned about their faith and foster dialogue among them about those experiences.

- Guide students in articulating the theological perspectives exemplified in their wide-ranging liturgical, spiritual, devotional, and cultural preferences.

- Be specific about how a particular student's comments broaden the view of the whole class and incorporate the thinking of diverse church members.

- Encourage critical thinking around issues of diversity and ask students to apply their understanding to their own lives and to pastoral situations.

- Make specific the implications for ministry in the various ministerial settings students will experience.

Developing skills:

- Generate ground rules for participation so that all students, especially those who are more insecure and introverted, can become confident enough to participate in discussion.

- Recognize the natural deference of students toward teachers that is inherent in some cultures, resulting in their reluctance to voice questions, make comments, or raise issues.

- Rearticulate or rephrase points expressed by a student to make them more universally applicable and understandable.

- Assign to students tasks such as looking for themes, noticing culture-specific variations in concepts or age-specific concerns about certain practices, and summarizing the main points of the discussion.

Evaluating progress:

- Invite students to write out any points made during the class that were unclear or confusing to them.

- Ask students from time to time what helps them feel engaged in the course content and what makes it difficult for them to enter into conversation.

- Arrange opportunities in informal settings for students to discuss topics of mutual concern, to participate in conversations that raise new questions, and to dialogue with different interest groups, for example, during small group luncheon conversations or voluntary gatherings.

PRINCIPLE 4. *Attempt to understand attitudes and pieties of incoming students.*

Many of today's students come to theological studies with a predetermined sense of how they plan to exercise their ministry, especially regarding their prayer and liturgical preferences. When working with these students, the issue is more one of attitude and less of theology. The belief expressed by some students that "people who disagree with me are not truly Catholic" is disconcerting for any faculty member. Direct confrontation with students who assert this often proves unsatisfactory, but exposing students to a wide range of theological content, prayer, and worship can be helpful.

Analyzing what causes students to be resistant to learning and opening them to a broader view of church tradition are essential. Many can learn to see the wisdom of flexibility for the sake of the community when it comes to styles of prayer. Although some students are so rigid that nothing will touch their patterns and practices, others are amenable to change when they are exposed to a broader range of ideas. As they do their analysis of students, faculty members need to be alert to their own biases so that they can keep in clear view the goal of ensuring students' capacity to serve the church's mission.

PRACTICES:

Expanding opportunities:

- Be attentive to the personal pieties present among entering students.

- Encourage students to describe their preferred devotions and pious practices and how they came to adopt them.

- Introduce students to a broad range of church prayer and devotions, both liturgical and personal.

- Seek to broaden and deepen those pieties through conversation and study of the universal church's mainstream traditions.

- Emphasize a personal encounter with Christ as a basis for all private prayer and communal worship.

Analyzing positions:

- Determine by oral and written assignments and by classroom observations whether the major issue with students is rigidity in their positions that could inhibit ministry to the entire people of God.

- Recognize the fact that new students may display a hostile closed attitude because they misinterpret data and miss clear distinctions in written materials due more to poor reading comprehension than to ideology.

- Bring to the surface students' unacknowledged internal dissonance, both cognitive and affective, with what is being taught.

- Uncouple theological stances (conservative/liberal) from dismissive attitudes toward positions that differ from those held by students.

- Recognize one's own predilection for certain kinds of religious practices.

- Hold students accountable to respond appropriately to institutional expectations by periodically reviewing their progress.

- Stress the importance of entering into the worship life of whatever ministry situation the future may present.

- Vary spiritual exercises within the formation community.

- Insist on music that reflects the breadth of the tradition.

- Arrange for students to worship at a church of another culture several times each year.

Develop a Suitable Curriculum and Appropriate Teaching Methods

PRINCIPLE 1. *Present a panoramic survey of the theological tradition in all its breadth and diversity.*

The starting point for beneficial teaching and learning is a curriculum that addresses the learning styles and theological backgrounds of students. Those who are preparing for ministry are more likely to engage their studies if they have confidence that they are being taught "what the church teaches." Yet difficulty arises when they define this as a narrow, static set of propositions rather than as a broad, dynamic body of living faith. Faculty need to explain carefully their intent to offer numerous perspectives within the tradition, while at the same time recognizing the limits of time and the shortcomings in students' backgrounds that might mitigate against a fuller presentation. One faculty member, for example, used role-play to illustrate a position by assigning one student to take on the persona of someone who hesitates to adopt the historical-critical method. This practice seemed to consolidate the "opposition" into a single voice, thereby relieving several others of the felt-need to quarrel.

Since their future ministry is at stake, students need examples of how to adapt their ministry to varied situations and diverse congregations. A useful approach is through historical studies where they learn how their predecessors dealt with difference and controversy. Through examining the ways the faith is lived in different cultures and how it has been adapted over time, students begin to see the significance of interpreting the tradition in light of culture. For example, one faculty member asked a Mexican seminarian who brought an annotated Spanish Bible to class to share, on occasion, the wisdom contained in that commentary. The curriculum must be explicit about including these dimensions.

PRACTICES:

Teaching for comprehensiveness:

- Survey the intellectual interests of students when they enter by asking them to write their expectations of the seminary's curriculum.

- Incorporate as constitutive elements in the theological curriculum the depth and breadth of the church's tradition, including the church as it is today.

- Provide courses that reflect both traditional and contemporary concerns.

- Cover as many sides of a theme or issue as possible when presenting material, avoiding a single perspective.

- Prioritize the key diverse ideas and opinions to present in light of time constraints and the capacity of students.

Interpreting the tradition:

- Show how theologians have dealt with controversial and opposing positions throughout the history of the church.

- Expand students' experience of church by illustrating how various cultures have interpreted the tradition.

- Deepen student understanding of the development of doctrine in the church.

- Inventory current curricular requirements and match them with the ministerial contexts in which students will be working.

- Recognize that the acculturation of students to new material and new ideas takes time.

PRINCIPLE 2. *Determine desired competencies and develop the curriculum according to varying levels of intellectual ability and educational experiences.*

This principle shifts from the content of the curriculum to the students. If faculty are clear about what they consider necessary competencies, they need next to match course objectives with the learning needs and backgrounds of the students. If students with learning problems are enrolled, remedial studies will be required. In some cases English as a second language will be an issue. Since students with varied intellectual capabilities and preferences for learning will be in the same classes, faculty have the challenging task of responding to students at every level. Faculty awareness of learning styles can help them adapt their teaching methods accordingly.

Beyond these special considerations, the academic program should not stand alone, isolated from other areas of formation. Faculty can assist students as they attempt to integrate and apply their learning to their own faith life, to their interactions with other students, and to their pastoral placements. If homiletics and Scripture faculty teach a course jointly, students can experience how to move from a Scripture text to a well-articulated homily, or a canon lawyer working with a sacramental theologian can demonstrate the application of legal principles to real parish situations. The more faculty members synthesize and coordinate teaching, the more likely students will gain the competency to do the same. Example is a powerful teacher when attempting to lead students from varied educational backgrounds to common integrated practice.

PRACTICES:

Determining competencies:

- Engage faculty in discussions of learning expectations they have for students.
- Communicate frequently to students the expectations of the faculty.
- Take into account the intellectual profile of students and their educational backgrounds in deciding the content and pace of requirements.
- Consider the cultural heritage both of students and of recipients of their future ministry when deciding on competencies.
- Integrate requirements related to all aspects of formation, not just courses, when developing lists of proficiencies.

Adapting teaching methods:

- Identify different learning styles among students by surveying them as to how they believe they learn best.

- Try to teach by imagining that you have never heard the material you are presenting.

- Connect what is being taught with what students already know by building on students' experiences of faith or conversion.

- Ask students to bring to class an insight or a question about the assigned reading and at the end of a class ask students to list three things they have learned, what surprised them, and what needs to be clarified.

- Encourage students to form study groups outside of class; minutes from these groups can be turned in for credit.

- Schedule one-on-one conferences with students in connection with term projects and use the opportunity to discern how effective your teaching methods are for them.

Developing curriculum:

- Consider the overall curriculum as a process that informs the way of doing theology, not simply as placement and content of individual courses.

- Reconfigure theological departments or areas, develop new categories, change placement of courses, and add new core and elective courses as needed.

- Manifest the synthesis or complementary elements in theological development in the subject matter being taught.

- Draw on interdisciplinary dialogue among faculty and interdisciplinary teaching of courses as a means of enhancing the curriculum.

PRINCIPLE 3. *Portray theological diversity as a resource and asset for classroom pedagogy, for theological education, and for future ministry.*

With a carefully articulated academic curriculum in place, faculty can demonstrate how attention to and awareness of diversity enhance learning. Regular, almost constant, attention must be paid to the wealth of insight that can be gained from theological perspectives arising from many sources. In the classroom setting, student contributions reflecting a particular cultural interpretation should be given special attention. Through practice and repetition, students can grasp how much of an asset these observations will be in ministry.

PRACTICES:

Raising awareness:

- Enable students to see theological diversity within the tradition as a constant source of dynamism in the faith by using examples, case studies, and other concrete illustrations.

- Reflect diversity in course syllabi, lectures, discussions, case studies, bibliographies, and assignments.

Employing appropriate methods:

- Use a variety of techniques in the classroom that in themselves reflect the giftedness of those with diverse cultural and theological backgrounds.

- Require students to articulate their own theological perspectives and to express their personal analyses and responses to others.

- Ask students to describe a liturgy or devotion they have admired or appreciated and how they believe this practice would be received by various types of congregations.

Ministerial Identity and Practice

Having considered diversity from the point of view of the classroom, attention now turns to ways faculty can ensure application of principles about diversity in ministry. This challenge centers on expansiveness of perspective and awareness of context. Emphasis on the whole tradition and on incorporation of a broad spectrum of patterns and practices in ministerial settings helps students become aware of their own cultural backgrounds in relation to the broader church. Forming students in the context of the faith communities in which they will be ministering is a practical way for them to recognize differences between their cultures and those of the communities in which ministry is taking place.

PRINCIPLE 1. *Prepare authentic ministers who work out of the whole tradition of the church in each ministerial situation.*

Augmenting some of the principles related to curriculum and teaching, this principle emphasizes the practice of ministry. The broad overview includes awareness of historical, cultural developments affecting religious practice and sensibilities as well as present-day ministry in a religiously diverse world. When students engage in pastoral field education, the effectiveness of the curriculum becomes apparent. This stage of integration, described more fully in the next chapter, is the goal of theological education for ministry.

PRACTICES:

Acquiring a broad overview of ministerial competence:

- Help students identify how the entire tradition contributes to ministerial effectiveness.

- Show that diversity has a historical basis, beginning in the earliest times when missionaries engaged the cultures they evangelized.

- Structure the formation program to help students recognize and name ways in which study and spirituality come together in ministry.

- Expand student awareness of the ecumenical and inter-religious dimension of the church's ministry by arranging opportunities for dialogue with other faith communities.

- Ask students to describe a priest or lay ecclesial minister whom they have admired and would like to imitate and then identify the skills or qualities that person uses in ministerial practice.

Considering the ministerial situation:

- Respect the ministerial agenda of students as they begin their theological studies.

- Surface these agendas by asking students to identify their ministerial expectations in writing and by discussing how those expectations relate to the cultural context for ministry.

- Provide clear, constructive, and critical feedback to students about their ministerial agenda as they progress through their programs.

- Help students to see how their efforts to establish their own sense of ministerial or priestly identity affect their ministerial practices.

PRINCIPLE 2. *Incorporate a broad spectrum of patterns and practices in preparing students for ministry.*

Faculty members with varied backgrounds and broad experience themselves are central to implementing this principle. In their teaching and interaction with students, they need to model breadth and inclusivity of both persons and ideas. The total institutional environment also plays a role in providing a range of liturgies (including musical styles), in carefully selected artwork, and in developing the library collection. Attentiveness to multiple expressions of worship and varying needs for pastoral care should be highlighted throughout the curriculum. In Scripture courses, for example, the professor can ask such questions as: "How does this passage affect our concern for the poor?" or "Who is included in this parable and who is left out?" Another relatively effortless way of tapping into a rich array of resources is through the use of technology and its access to the worldwide web. A later chapter illustrates this in depth.

PRACTICES:

Integrating diverse practices:

- Coach faculty on how to be models for collaborative and inclusive ministry in the ways they incorporate all students in their teaching processes.

- Include reference to the entire church in all its theological and cultural diversity, not just one segment.

- Design explicit course expectations that guide students in integrating what they learn in classes with their ministerial experiences.

- Promote effective liturgy with a responsible approach to church directives such as the *General Instruction on the Roman Missal.*

- Form a student liturgy committee to work with a faculty director of liturgy that mirrors the diversity of the community.

Expanding opportunities:

- Establish a comprehensive social concerns program that brings students into many sectors of the larger community.

- Allocate time for seminars on ministerial priesthood and lay ecclesial ministry that are rigorous, open, and demanding, as well as inclusive of examples from many cultures and settings.

- Explore the potential use of technology in designing classroom pedagogy that broadens students' exposure to ministerial practices in various types of communities.

PRINCIPLE 3. *Inculcate awareness of each student's own culture and demonstrate its relationship to ministry.*

Two dynamics are essential in promoting awareness of the impact of culture on ministry: self-understanding and relationship to individuals who model inclusive ministry. Self-understanding begins in the classroom where teachers provide an environment that requires attentiveness to one's own culture as seen in contrast to others. Through readings, videos, guest lecturers, and reflection on the anthropological dimensions of ministry, students' awareness grows. During ministerial fieldwork, the theoretical becomes practical as students engage with an array of cultural expressions of worship and Christian life.

PRACTICES:

Gaining self-understanding:

- Teach students how to recognize the importance of knowing one's own culture as they gain awareness of how cultures work and interact.

- Help students practice openness to those they encounter in their pastoral placements by shaping classroom experiences that promote interaction and authentic dialogue among students and with the faculty members.

- Increase faculty awareness of cultural and intellectual diversity so they will be able to manifest leadership in dealing with differences in their courses, workshops, curriculum development, and other aspects of school life.

Seeking models:

- Invite into the classroom people who are living models of dialogue with diverse cultures and situations.

- Make use of a range of ministerial settings in which students spend time so that they learn to recognize the impact of different needs and interests of people.

- Teach students how to adapt their styles and methods of ministry to match the needs of the people they serve.

- Help students identify their own model of ministry and how this shapes their expectations and ways of interacting in pastoral placements.

PRINCIPLE 4. *Form pastoral theologians for ministry in their particular context or faith community.*

This fourth principle reinforces some of the practical suggestions already mentioned, but now focuses exclusively on the pastoral context. To the extent that faculties understand and experience the situations in which their students will eventually minister, they will have greater success in helping students interact effectively in those settings. Classroom references to the demands placed on the pastor and staff in differing types of parishes can help students become more attuned to expectations. Asking pastors, staff, and parishioners about how well newly assigned or hired ministers are performing in their roles can assist the school in evaluating its teaching.

PRACTICES:

Relating to pastoral contexts:

- Demonstrate how the context of ministry offers a frame of reference that contributes to decisions about appropriate ministry.

- Articulate the complexity of ministry and the numerous ways people come to conversion.

- Increase the consonance between the experience of priests and parish staffs and the competencies included in theological formation.

- Use examples in class that have application in ministry.

- Ensure that students, as well as faculty, have knowledge of the contexts in which they as seminarians or lay ecclesial ministers will work.

- Give students tools that will help them know what data are required to understand the contextual demands of particular types of ministerial service.

Evaluating pastoral contexts:

- Ask persons with whom students interact in a ministerial setting how effective students are in exercising their ministry.

- Ascertain from pastors and parishioners how well recently ordained deacons and priests and new lay ministers are performing their responsibilities in the parish.

Faculty Development

Previous sections highlighted some of the ways faculty are responding to current challenges in teaching and learning for the church's ministries in seminaries and theologates. In light of the considerable changes in student characteristics, faculty need to consciously build a sense of collegiality and develop an air of confidence in meeting the new situation. These suggestions for faculty support their work to advance the mission of their schools, to develop confidence in doing their work, and to advance their skills in dealing with increasingly diverse classrooms.

PRINCIPLE 1. *Build collegial effort among faculty members as they advance the mission of the school.*

The diverse student bodies of most theologates require a genuine transformation in faculty approaches to teaching. This type of adaptation is difficult to manage alone, but becomes more possible as faculty collegially see the effort as a way of responding to the evolving mission of the school. Raising awareness of the connection between adapting to diversity and forwarding the mission of a school is an important task for deans and other administrators. They can provide opportunities and incentives for faculty members to advance their capacity to teach an ever-changing student body and thus further the primary mission of the school. The resources for improvement are often already present within the faculty who need only a platform to share their insights with colleagues.

PRACTICES:

Advancing the mission:

- Build a sense of collegiality among the faculty by taking concrete steps to call the faculty to mutual responsibility for one another's growth.

- Arrange focused discussion where individual faculty members articulate how their teaching, research, and writing contributes to an understanding of the mission of the school.

- Ask faculty members to articulate in their sabbatical proposals how the sabbatical will contribute to the mission of the school generally and specifically to the content and pedagogy of their courses.

Sharing insights:

- Provide occasions for faculty to express to each other their theological foundations and understandings, for example, during annual off-campus retreats or periodic faculty dinners preceded by facilitated discussions.

- Include as a regular part of faculty meetings a brief time for faculty members, on a rotating basis, to report on a meeting, conference, article, or book that has aided their understanding of diversity and how it applies to the school.

- Ask faculty members to include in their annual reports examples of successful adaptation to an aspect of diversity they have encountered and then compile these findings as a resource for the full faculty.

PRINCIPLE 2. *Build faculty confidence and experience by helping them develop competence in dealing with diversity.*

Adaptation of teaching and learning to respond to a student body whose diversity is exhibited in theological and learning style differences takes energy, time, and courage. When faculty disclose their discomfort about articulating their own beliefs to one another and then gradually develop confidence in sharing their deeply held convictions, they are likely to experience a sense of relief and a renewed capacity to work effectively with students. New forums for mutual learning can also be helpful, for example, arranging for discussions of theological and cultural diversity with students and faculty together. The faculty member becomes in such instances both learner and teacher—a learner as students share how well their educational experience suits them and a teacher in mentoring students toward greater theological and cultural sensitivity toward those who are different from them. Further, it is useful to organize field excursions to parishes representing strongly diverse groups and ways of thinking. Trips to the countries of origin of students and study abroad with students are rich sources for mutual learning.

PRACTICES:

Developing confidence:

- Design ways to practice forthright discussion about theological differences while respecting faculty hesitancy and reluctance.

- Provide incentives, such as course releases, to prepare new methods of teaching and ways of interacting with students that can contribute to the success of the students' formation.

- Show how faculty model being inquiring learners by becoming more informed about their students who are educationally, intellectually, and religiously diverse.

- Consider short-term study tours in the countries of origin of students and/or of those to whom graduates will be ministering.

Increasing faculty skills:

- Build the faculty's sense of collegiality through interaction and discussion of common concerns.

- Arrange for presentations on issues of theological diversity to create a forum in which true dialogue and a search for understanding prevail.

- Organize opportunities to engage in conversations about diversity with students.

- Participate in ongoing faculty development by focusing on broader concerns, especially as they are manifested in ministry settings.

Summary and Conclusions

Over the past quarter century, the changes in the type of students attending seminaries and schools of theology have created exciting opportunities and demanding circumstances for students, faculty, and administrators. Because of significant modifications in immigration laws, racial/ethnic diversity has increased especially among ordination candidates, but also among lay students and members of the church generally. Depending somewhat on the location and admissions policies of schools, a few have experienced only moderate changes in their student body composition. Many have undergone a greater but manageable degree of change, and a few feel they have reached what they perceive to be a saturation point in absorbing cultural and theological differences among students. In any case, the fruits of the discussions at Keystone yielded principles and practices to assist the teaching and learning process during this time of transition.

Faculty and administrators have discovered, through consultation, trial and error, and responses of students, the necessity of adjusting their methodologies, content, and the environment of the school and classroom. Perhaps of greatest importance, they have taken into account in deeper ways the societal and religious shifts affecting the very identity of Catholics and their understanding of the church. To adapt, schools have created more welcoming and hospitable settings by appreciating generational differences, especially as these affect theological positions. They have developed appropriate curricula, teaching methods, and formational goals relative to the ministerial requirements in the future. More vigorous faculty development has enhanced the communal identity of faculty and their confidence in teaching students with a wide range of theological and educational backgrounds. Faculty participation in the cultural worlds of their students and in the ministry settings where graduates will be placed has helped build their knowledge and skills in the teaching and learning process. While diversity creates enormous shifts in "how we do things here," the attentiveness of faculty members to what needs to be done has reaped significant benefit to the understanding of what it means to teach and to learn.

Principles and Practices of Diversity for Pastoral Settings

While this book emerges from patterns and changes in theological education for ministry, principles and practices raised in this chapter have applicability in parishes.

• Create a Hospitable Environment

Parish leaders can help people feel welcome by gaining an understanding of who comprises the congregation and what the church means to them. This information may be gathered through informal conversations, the wise use of focus groups, and even a full parish census. A second step in creating a hospitable environment would be to make clear that all are welcome. This stance requires that members actually practice respect for one another's views and opinions and put the most positive interpretation on them. The pastor, staff, and lay leaders must be models of this behavior in all that they do.

– Attempt to recognize who constitutes the membership of the parish and gain an understanding of their attitudes and values regarding the Church.

– Recognize that the meaning of Catholic identity and resulting expectations of the parish are major issues for parishioners and both vary significantly among members.

– Make diversity acceptable, even desirable, by acknowledging and highlighting the gifts of persons from different cultural, religious, and educational backgrounds.

– Establish and maintain an atmosphere of safety and trust in which all persons respect each other's opinions in all their encounters.

• Develop Ministries Appropriate to a Particular Parish

The pastor and other staff ministers should search out and identify as many cultural, educational, philosophical, and age-specific needs as they can and draw on them in designing programs and liturgical services. If diversity is portrayed as a resource and asset, parishioners are more likely to respond with pride than antipathy toward fresh approaches to liturgy and other parish programs.

– Present the breadth and diversity of the Catholic theological tradition in all aspects of worship, education, and preaching.

– Communicate frequently how the diversity of the parish is a resource and asset to the development of ministries.

– Determine desired ministerial outcomes and develop the formational and educational programs according to varying needs of parishioners.

• **Establish Clear Norms for Ministerial Practice**

Reflecting the whole of Catholic tradition is essential if ministers are to be attentive to as many differences among parishioners as possible. Pastoral ministers themselves, however, may lack the preparation needed to do this well. This lacuna may mean finding or creating professional continuing education opportunities for those responsible for parish programs so they can grow in their skillfulness to incorporate new approaches in their ministry. A key element in this ongoing development as a minister is consciousness of how one's own cultural and religious experience influences what one considers "normative."

– Prepare staff to work out of the whole tradition of the church in each ministerial program.

– Incorporate a broad spectrum of patterns and practices rather than one approach to worship, education, and pastoral service.

– Inculcate awareness of how each staff member's own culture and experiences relate to the ministry they provide.

– Develop the skillfulness of staff members in reading the context of the faith community in which they are working.

– Actively encourage collegial commitment of the staff to further the mission of the parish in its diversity.

– Provide opportunities to develop staff competence in dealing with diversity.

CHAPTER 3

Seeing Things Whole:
A Reflection on Integration

Introduction

In an essay on transformative education and adult learning, Patricia Cranton describes an experience familiar to those who teach. Over the course of a semester, a student in her class on teaching theory had been fairly quiet and showed a low level of interest in the material. When the student asked a question, it was often rhetorical in character as though he had some private assumption he needed to protect. In a discussion one day, Cranton notes, she observed a physical change come over the student. He sat up straighter and had a look of astonishment on his face. "Andrew announced that he saw, accepted, and clearly understood the shades of gray existing in knowledge about teaching."[1]

The moments we have as teachers when this sort of immediate, tangible breakthrough occurs for a student are delightful. A student's visibly "getting it"—seeing how ideas come together and help cast light on the meaning of one's assumptions and operative theories—captures what many faculty seek to foster. Every student may not manifest that moment in the same way as Cranton's student, but faculty at the Keystone Conferences who were concerned about integration would recognize the phenomenon. The lack of apparent integration was a source of frustration and concern. They were good teachers, dedicated to their disciplines, concerned about their students, and focused on equipping graduates for insightful ministry in various areas of church life. For many, however, students were not often sitting up straighter with looks of astonishment on their faces.

Patricia Cranton would suggest that in part the expectation itself is misleading. It is misleading if one presumes that a teacher is in the

49

position of commanding integration to occur at a particular moment in the formation process. There are ways in which schools can organize the experience of learning so that the elements of integration are present and so that students have the skills and *experience of exercising those skills* in a way that manifests the transformative effects of integration. Unlike learning the key points of the christological controversies, the arguments that support a dogmatic principle, or the canons that refer to the role of the laity in the church, integration has no set content. It is a complex reality whose different facets challenge the work of theological education.

Integration, then, is not simply a theoretical issue or an issue of pedagogical speculation. It has to do with an understanding of formation in which the whole is in fact greater than the parts. Too often, many faculty members report, students see little connection among key activities in a curriculum—that is, being able to pass exams and write acceptable research papers, showing sufficient aptitude for pastoral work, and demonstrating growth as a person grounded in a healthy spirituality. This disconnection is what drives concerns for seeking ways to teach for integration. For the purposes of this chapter, integration is defined as *a formative process that engages students in traditions of theological knowledge, pastoral practice, and Christian identity as they examine, re-interpret, and commit themselves to a worldview that bears the deep imprint of those traditions.*

The movement implied by this definition relies on the active reexamination of one's assumptions about theology, the church, ministry, spirituality, piety, and one's self. It presumes a permeability among knowledge, practice, and identity. Without such a permeability the student entering the seminary or theological school leaves with little more than an ability to argue more strongly why she or he was right in the first place. Moreover, the process exceeds a particular moment—like that of Cranton's student—but unfolds over time so that integration for a student beginning formation will look quite different three years later when she graduates or ten years later as she establishes herself in pastoral ministry.

While integration in theological education and formation is an aspiration for many faculties, there are not many objective definitions. Perhaps one of the most general guidelines comes from the Association of Theological Schools. Its accrediting standards frame integration in terms of the interrelationship of the parts of a curriculum. One of its general standards, for instance, calls for an approach to teaching and learning that fosters, "in addition to the acquisition of knowledge, the capacity to understand and assess one's tradition and identity, and to integrate materials from various theological disciplines and modes of instructional engagement in ways that enhance ministry and cultivate emotional and spiritual maturity" (3.1.1.3). Two standards for the master of divinity address this approach more specifically:

> A.3.1.1.3. Instruction in these areas shall be conducted so as to indicate their interdependence with each other and with other areas of the curriculum, and their significance for the exercise of pastoral leadership.
>
> A.3.1.4.2. The program shall ensure a constructive relationship among courses dealing primarily with the practice of ministry and courses dealing primarily with other subjects.

Principles of Integration

Wide agreement is present among those with distinctively different philosophies of learning that integration is at the heart of education and formation. People who immerse themselves in an educational experience that is by intention formative should theoretically emerge from that process somehow transformed—not by magic but by the slow, cumulative impact of seeing and experiencing the web of connections among ideas, assumptions, and the discovery of new angles of vision. Faculties rightly believe that their work is to create the opportunities for learners to encounter knowledge, belief, and practice in ways that raise to a new level of consciousness what it means to see things whole.

When integration works, the separate parts of the curriculum that give order and sequence to a course of studies lose their sharp edges and begin to meld into a new vision of how the world, church, and ministry interrelate. At some point, what a learner knows moves from mechanical acquisition to reflexive response, and the practices of professional ministry are no longer the application of certain routines or sequences of steps but the fluid artistry of one who understands that beneath practice runs the electric current of theological wisdom. This movement means that the new vision is not just another construct, but something that changes the individual at his or her core. Yet, all this lies behind a door that faculty cannot force a learner to pass through. The mystery of integration is that it has everything to do with what a faculty strives to achieve even as it is beyond its direct control.

As the opening anecdote of this chapter illustrates, someone who has immersed himself or herself in years of disciplinary study and reflection rightly longs for the moment when students "get it" and move from banking data to asking questions that take data deeper and deeper into meaning. The concerns of Keystone participants often centered on the fact that such integration happened only fitfully or not at all or that the efforts to move beyond simple accumulation or reproduction of information were met with resistance or disinterest.

Integration in Catholic theological education for ministry, however, is not a one-dimensional phenomenon. While the definition of integration framed for this chapter is another angle on the discussions we find elsewhere—for example, the interrelationships among the intellectual, pastoral, personal, and spiritual formation components of a program in developing the capacity and character of individuals for pastoral leadership—any definition would fall short in capturing fully its different facets. Three principles, however, anchor pedagogical interventions faculty members and their formational colleagues can take if in fact they are concerned about creating an environment that fosters integration.

The first principle about integration is that it is a *benchmark* offering tangible evidence that a student sees at an acceptable level the interrelationships among classroom, chapel, ministry setting, and personal-spiritual counseling. As a benchmark, integration is the global outcome of the curriculum. The continual challenge is the need for ongoing redefinition of the benchmark in light of changing characteristics in each generation of learners and in light of a faculty's increasing critical insight into what members agree comprises an "integrated seminary or theological school" education. Some may argue that integration has transgenerational meaning, a universality one can track across time. That assumption—largely untested—can create unrealistic expectations or deep frustration when students do not look integrated in a certain way or in a way characteristic of another era.

It is a helpful practice for faculty members and all other teachers for whom integration is a benchmark of educational success to ask periodically, "What do integrated students look like? What can we expect from them in terms of how they respond to new ideas, pastoral dilemmas, and discussions that involve more than linking the right answer to the right question?"

Another principle of integration is that it is also a *process* that moves at different rates for different individuals. Because it is a process, it is only partially responsive to the structures and sequences established as normative for a school. Everyone takes certain courses, often in a similar sequence, completing fairly standard assignments intended to challenge and demonstrate their appropriation of important information. In between those formal activities are all the complex individual realities that affect one's ability to respond to integrative assumptions.

These individual realities include the *internal freedom* needed to respond to learning that "deconstructs" one's fundamental assumptions; the *prior knowledge* a person brings to a learning task; a *personal piety* that may see the demands of rational analysis as unnecessary or perhaps dangerous to one's faith claims; and an *instrumental understanding of religious vocation* that produces a tension between a desire for answers and tested strategies and a systematic exploration of ideas and principles for how one might act in an unfamiliar, unpredictable situation. Such dynamics weigh heavily on the unfolding of the integrative process. What theological faculties tend to lack is an understanding of how the process moves forward and what signs along the way suggest progress in all its variability. Later in this chapter there is a developmental understanding of the integrative process that can increase faculty members' skills in teaching for integration.

Keystone participants recognized that the transformative focus of integration is not a commodity and therefore able to be prescribed or contained by program requirements alone. Attention shifts from finding a formula that will produce integration as a product to a process with activities and practices that ground individuals in the intellectual disciplines, reflective skills, and spiritual dispositions for a lifetime of active commitment to the integrative process. In this regard, it is interesting to note how strongly integration figures in the U.S. Catholic Bishops' plan for ongoing formation of clergy:

> Integration is at the heart of ongoing formation, as priests grow in bringing together *who* they are and *what* they do. Their growth is really a growing integrity or connectedness of their ministry and their life.[2]

A third principle about integration is that it is an educational *strategy* that engages teachers and learners in purposeful action. For some students, integration is almost a reflex in their approach to learning. They are always asking the meta-questions, seeing the linkages between ideas, discerning their assumptions and those of their professors, and drawing conclusions that weave together various dimensions and threads of knowledge. They are not intimidated by intellectual complexity and have achieved a level of personal development that sets them free to be in the presence of new and challenging ways of thinking and responding. Such a group is a delight to teach. However, for the majority of students—students who are often bright and capable—their approaches to learning tend to be more sequential and discrete. They learn sets of data in different areas of knowledge and expect to be tested on their mastery of those data or demonstrate some measure of competency. Such students do not presume that these various sources of learning—whether from discipline to discipline or from the classroom to ministry placement or from spiritual formation to study—interact in ways that mutually inform each other.

For several years, for instance, a colleague facilitated the master of divinity integrative seminar, working in partnership with another member of the faculty and a local pastor. Using cases generated by the pastors, student discussion leaders presented their analysis of the dilemma and offered a theologically grounded pastoral response. It was the rare student who could do this in an "integrative" fashion. Most could offer a response that addressed the interpersonal and psychological elements in the situation. Most could refer to church law germane to the situation, and many would make reference to the new *Catechism of the Catholic Church* and the work of one or more theologians. What became apparent was that the integrative challenge posed by the seminar was many times happening for the first time. Students generally had not been asked to reflect on pastoral dilemmas, bringing to bear the wisdom of the church in their analysis of what to do in unique, unpredictable, and complex situations. Helping students get to this point is a strategic pedagogical practice that cultivates skillfulness one should expect from a learned professional.

These three principles of integration—as benchmark, process, and strategy—capture what sometimes seems like an elusive reality. The elusiveness results from a sobering fact that, even when integration is well defined, is approached as a developmental process, and nurtured through well-chosen strategic practices, integration cannot be forced. It depends on the readiness of students to respond to the opportunities offered to see things whole and to explore the relationships that exist among what one knows, what one can do, and who one is. Cultivating and supporting this readiness is the work of a teaching faculty. Responding is the responsibility of students themselves even though it may stretch them beyond their comfort zones.

One final general observation on integration is important. Integration happens at multiple levels simultaneously. People can appreciate that integration at the personal level is in fact dependent upon the individual working with grace and nature in responding to the opportunities education and formation offer. The environment for integration, however, is tangible and finds representation in the coherence of the curriculum in which the alignment of institutional goals balances the internal demands of an academic community for scholarly work with the external demands for people equipped to provide highly competent professional service. If the environment fails to model how parts of a reality fit together to form a whole, expectations for individuals to embrace the process of integration are undermined.

Integration and the Role of the Faculty

One of the insights emerging from the conversations at Keystone was that integration is as much about faculty as it is about students and strategic pedagogy. A faculty might be eloquent in defining its understanding of integration, and the curriculum can be jammed full of practices that foster integration without creating an integrative environment. Keystone participants pointed out that faculty members must model integration in their personal and professional lives. Brilliant professors who are indifferent to their treatment of students, sarcastic about pastoral life and its issues, ideologically narrow and defensive about their interpretations of the truth, or unable to articulate how the life of scholarship influences their own spiritualities compromise a school's efforts to encourage and support student integrative development. Faculty who demonstrate that the disciplines essential to integration do not really matter tacitly reinforce students' resistance to integration.

Another perspective on the significance of faculty modeling is that integration cannot be isolated in certain courses, areas, or departments of the school. Indeed, those charged with pastoral and spiritual formation responsibilities have a particular opportunity to engage students in ways that deepen their capacity to achieve integration among the various facets of their education. A significant transformation in worldview implicit in integration and the level of skillfulness required to achieve an "integrative disposition" argue against concluding that courses like preaching or area requirements such as field education can stand alone. In fact, even integrative seminars at the completion of a program, despite their titles, are insufficient to bear the burden of developing a capacity for integration. Such seminars, it can be argued, should be places in which students demonstrate skills, knowledge, and abilities developed throughout the curriculum and modeled by all faculty.

Faculty development in this area of integration is no small matter. Long gone are the days when faculty members could describe their work as teaching a standard set of courses, continuing their own study, and serving the local church in various ways. As seminary and ministry formation have grown complex, so have the expectations of faculty. In work resulting from their participation in the Keystone Conferences, the faculty members of Notre Dame Seminary explored the tensions that seem to hold them as they carry out their responsibilities. The paradoxes they identified are not unique to their setting but provide a broader, fuller understanding of the challenges faculty face in being models for integration. Consider the following:

- We admit students with widely varied backgrounds AND
  we expect them all to perform like adult graduate students.

- We invite students to appreciate mystery AND
  we respond to their need for answers.

- We form the students in a culture AND
  we help them to remain open to other cultures.

- We are asked to be teachers AND
  we fulfill multiple other roles.

- We teach to engage gifted students AND
  we teach to support students struggling to learn.

- We want students to know traditional Church teaching AND
  we want them to think critically.

- We want to provide dynamic, interactive presentations AND
  we want to insure substantive coverage of content.

- We deal with what students feel should be expected of them AND
  we meet the expectations of the school and Church for formation.

These paradoxical tensions in theological education and their implications for faculty and the work of the school get insufficient attention.

As a result, expectations for faculty expand but the framework within which the institution thinks about faculty life does not. The modeling required of faculty that is essential to the effectiveness of the school tends to receive scant attention in how faculty life is structured. Apart from policies of hiring and retaining faculty, the issue of ongoing development of faculty must be reprioritized if the work of integration is to be advanced in significant ways.

Arriving at consensus about what integration means within a particular school, exploring pedagogical strategies that develop and cultivate readiness for integration, and identifying what reasonable signs one can look for as students respond to the opportunities offered them all require trust among faculty members. They require the ability to listen to perspectives that challenge one's assumptions about theological education and formation or that make one uncomfortable. They require an ability to make one's teaching transparent to colleagues so that mutual critique and affirmation enhance the skills of faculty as teachers. These are developmental challenges that must be part of any serious effort to make integration a benchmark of a school's educational efforts.

Five Principles for Faculty Development

Carolyn Jurkowitz, associate director for education of the Catholic Conference of Ohio and former public member on the Commission on Accrediting for the Association of Theological Schools, has been helpful in creating a set of principles that can engage a faculty's systematic thinking about integration as an educational practice.[3]

PRINCIPLE 1. *There is consensus among faculty members on what integration of learning looks like in graduates.*

This principle establishes an essential starting point for it particularizes integration within an educational, formative context focused on preparation for professional ministry. Many faculty claim they would know what integration in a student would look like. Articulating that "vision" begins to reveal both the diversity of perceptions and points of convergence. With consensus, however, a faculty can begin assessing the results of practices that more intentionally facilitate the integrative process for students.

PRINCIPLE 2. *All faculty members believe themselves responsible for fostering integration.*

After reaching consensus about the faculty's understanding of integration, someone on the faculty might still say, "That's not my job. That is why we have a director of field education [or the M.Div. seminar]." The responsibility for integration resides in the entire faculty without exception. The particulars of that responsibility can be negotiated but not the ultimate claims it makes on each member.

PRINCIPLE 3. *Faculty are able and willing to teach for integration, including assessing what they do, acting on the assessment data, and making changes in pedagogy as required.*

This principle has the character of an altar call. It is among the most difficult challenges a faculty as a body faces. Teaching in higher education has been privileged. Once one has demonstrated mastery of a field, one is given wide leeway in what one does in the privacy of one's own classroom. Student course evaluations can put pressure on faculty to alter some behaviors and make some accommodations to student complaints. This principle calls for a level of competence in the classroom for which a faculty member is held accountable and which is often countercultural.

PRINCIPLE 4. *Structures are available to facilitate the capacity of faculty to teach for integration and to assess their efforts.*

Faculty development in the area of integration cannot be relegated to a discussion at a faculty meeting from time to time. That falls short of the direct action needed to help faculty assess their practice, receive the coaching they need to consider new or enhanced ways of teaching their subjects, and have the time this attentiveness to their practice requires. Academic deans need to shift the distribution of their work to favor resourcing their colleagues in teaching development. Evaluations for promotion and tenure could include various ways of helping faculty persons examine their teaching and receive peer feedback that augments other sources of assessment including student course evaluations and teacher-led classroom assessment. The escalation of the role of teaching development does not challenge the importance of scholarly development in one's field. It does re-position teaching to a more central role in the life of a school and the structures it creates to assist faculty in achieving what it is trying to accomplish.

PRINCIPLE 5. *Pedagogical practices encourage the development of student capacity for integration.*

At Keystone, participants identified various actions that they felt advanced the work of integration. Some had to do with what happened in the classroom. Others were more general and dealt with creating an environment where faculty members could develop a sense of teaching a curriculum rather than offering several courses in a field over which a member had a proprietary right. A brief discussion of these recommendations follows this section. The point is that eventually the conversation turns to what one actually does instructionally. There is a robust literature describing nearly fifty years of experiment, research, and critique about adult learning and critical pedagogy. Much of it emerges from education at the college level or from independent adult learning programs. This material is an insufficiently tapped resource as theological faculties try to determine, not what to teach in terms of Scripture, dogma, liturgy, and other subjects, but how one can teach in ways that engage learners for content mastery and integration.[4]

Teaching for Integration

Syllabi Discussions. What are some of the practices that can help faculties advance the work of integration as discussed in this essay? The starting place for many Keystone participants was dialogue among faculty members about what they are teaching. This exercise seems so obvious, yet it is surprising how many times it is an overlooked practice. Some of the neglect results from the pressures of time and some from the fear of faculty to expose what they do to peer critique. As faculty become more aware of what is being taught throughout the curriculum, they are able to identify ways in which requirements, expectations, cross-referencing, and use of similar resources and bibliographies can help students begin to see connections among what they are learning. Faculty, for example, could create assignments that span two or more courses in ways that would provide tangible experience for students of how discrete areas of knowledge impact and influence each other. Knowing what is happening in all the courses students are taking enables the faculty to identify more intentional ways of fostering integration in addition to the traditional research paper.

Team Teaching. Teachers working across disciplines collaboratively have an opportunity to model how integration of ideas works and how the process "looks" as team members argue, question, and build on each other's ideas. For team teaching to work, faculty members need to avoid the unit approach in which one teacher teaches his subject for several weeks, another teacher teaches her unit, and the course concludes with some shared use of the remaining weeks in the term. True team teaching is labor intensive and time consuming. Its benefits, however, make the costs worthwhile.

Attention to Learning Needs/Styles. The research on learning style differences has significantly eroded any notion that learning is a single-track phenomenon. Regarding integration, attention to learning style differences widens access to understanding by enabling individuals opportunities to enter the conversation in a way that is most productive for them. This reality does not mean that a teacher needs to create ten different course designs to accommodate learning style differences. It does mean considering style in designing a course so that at different times different style preferences are exercised. A very simple example is to alternate lecture with individual or small group tasks, theoretical explanations with opportunities to apply theory to practice, and focusing on the big picture with attention to details. Adult learners can come to adapt their preferences to a variety of learning situations. Enabling them to work at least some of the time from their preferred learning styles simply helps them build capacity for learning "out of preference" while it gives them ways to think from different angles about new ideas and concepts. One of the many benefits of educational technology has been its utility in responding to learning style differences.

Use of Critical Incidents and Cases. This practice has a long history of helping students move out of a compartmentalized way of thinking. Well-constructed and facilitated critical incidents or cases challenge a student to see how a response drawn from Scripture, church teaching, the varied perspectives offered by theologians, the requirements of canon law, and the psycho-social dynamics of personal and communal life interrelate in interpreting what is occurring in a particular time within a particular set of circumstances. Case studies and critical incidents, because they resituate good thinking within a context that is often messy and ambiguous, sharpen the student's ability to move back and forth among various domains of knowing.

Classroom Research. This relatively new practice supplements the limited usefulness of end-of-term course evaluations by providing a formative tool for improving teaching. If the focus of teaching is learning, then the benefits of monitoring the progress of learning as it happens seem self-evident. Classroom research is a set of relatively straightforward techniques an instructor uses periodically throughout a course to gain insight into student learning.[5] An example would be the "One-Minute Paper." At the end of a class period, the instructor asks students to spend one minute identifying the most important idea, question, or issue raised. The instructor collects the papers and evaluates their content, determining what students seem to be gaining and where key ideas are being missed. In the next meeting of the class, the instructor highlights progress being made and indicates what she will do to address areas in which there seems to be lack of clarity or understanding. Classroom assessment techniques are ideal for enabling faculty to observe, assess, and encourage the integration process.

Interdisciplinary Resources. The use of arts, humanities, and social sciences as resources for learning is another way to help students enrich and deepen the ways they see how things fit together. This pedagogical practice provides a more holistic viewpoint on knowledge that draws on ideas stimulating student imagination and uses all their senses. Examples might be visiting museums and arts galleries, taking field trips, and inviting in leaders in other professions or from other disciplines to reflect on theological questions from their perspectives.

Attention to Stages in Adult Development. Research on adult development can be useful as faculties consider ways of working with students and engaging them more intentionally in the integrative process. William Bridges offers an example of how developmental considerations may play out in a learning situation.[6] Drawing on the earlier work of Van Gennep and his own twenty years of guiding adults through life transitions, Bridges has confirmed a three-phased pattern: separation, a period of neutrality, and then re-incorporation. The phases are fairly self-explanatory. The major transitions in adult life involve separation from former ways well defined and bounded by norms, expectations, and reactions that predict the course of a day and its outcomes. Leaving all that behind involves disenchantment with its helpfulness, disengagement with its rhythms, disconnection with the identity it provided, and disillusionment with its agency as a force in one's life. Separation leaves one in a liminal space to discover a new way that, once gained, leads one into incorporation in a new phase of meaningful life. Consider that pattern in relation to a student who decided in midlife to become a priest or to prepare for fulltime ministry. By the time this person begins classes an entire psychodrama has occurred entailing the separation from one way of living, a period of discernment, and the incorporation into a "new way of being" as a seminarian or ministry student. In such a scenario, the notion of deconstruction-reconstruction of a new worldview, not unfamiliar in graduate education, can become an obstruction to learning. The students are coming to seminary or degree study as part of their response of being reincorporated into a new way of being. Having already experienced a major transition, they are not interested in having their views deconstructed but are looking for ways that will confirm their discernment of a ministerial call—of being incorporated into a new identity. Integration may well be what the students need, but it will occur in ways far different than for the student for whom enrolling in seminary or graduate study is his or her initial act of separation.

Attentiveness to adult development requires rethinking the role of experience as a factor in learning. Adults returning to graduate study and ministry formation enter the process with a reservoir of experience that dramatically impacts the ways in which they receive, analyze, and incorporate new ideas. Integrative pedagogies need to take seriously the extent to which adults use their experience to test and evaluate new ideas or propositions. This process is ideologically neutral in that, whatever the theological inclinations, the experienced adult looks at what a faculty member is teaching against what she or he already "knows" to be true. Building linkages to this reservoir of experience in ways that acknowledge the significance of what the student knows while inviting the student to look at that experience from a different angle of vision enables the process of integration to unfold.

Obviously, these pedagogical strategies only sample the wide array of what is available. What began at the Keystone Conferences continued to develop as participating teams returned home. With their colleagues, many faculties began to talk about what they do pedagogically—what methods they use or have tested to achieve the sort of deep learning associated with integration. It is in such conversations that faculty members discover the secret of developing into skilled pedagogues: listen to the people who share the work. As faculty learn to talk with one another about teaching, they begin to discover that in their midst are exceptional teachers; that the practices they engage as relatively common and plain are innovations to others; that the failures they have experienced have within them lessons that open up new strategies and approaches. Talk about teaching has for too long been subdued or relegated to an occasional workshop. If the work of integration is to advance, the formative and informative work of the faculty in the classroom and other learning settings needs to move to the heart of what a faculty does together.

The Role of Students in the Integrative Process

The focus on the role of faculty in integration is important because it is the faculty who sets the agenda and plans the curriculum. Faculty members have the power, and so their role in fostering integration is significant. At the same time, as powerful as the faculty might be and as diligent as many faculty members are in promoting readiness for integration, they cannot command it to happen. In the end, it is the student who controls whether he or she brings together the various dimensions of ministry formation and sees the world whole.

There are certain aptitudes, dispositions, or qualities that orient students to the integrative process. That said, it is important to note that some students are better at integration sooner than others and some will respond more readily than others. Some students are internally free of the need to cling to one certain way of framing the world while others take longer to test alternative ways and to deepen their capacity to consider other angles of vision. Christa Klein, a member of the Keystone leadership team, identified what she called "virtues for integration": wisdom, balance, purity of heart, wholeness, and discipline.[7] These are attributes that students need to acquire and cultivate as part of their commitment to the integrative process.

The faculty at Saint Meinrad School of Theology expanded on Dr. Klein's list in light of their experience with students.[8] Their list of virtues for integration began with *humility*, the ability to recognize what one does not know and to respect those who do know. Faculty members rightfully deserve recognition that their years of study and research equip them with more than "just one more opinion." Students also need to have a *love of learning* that kindles a desire to get behind and beneath the answer to a question. Wanting to know the answer to a question is an appropriate initial motivation for learning. Wanting to understand the answer rooted in a deep wisdom breathes life into what could be sterile and inert. The *willingness to risk* is at the heart of critical thinking. Integration short-circuits when the process of learning must squeeze through the narrow door of a predetermined answer. Without risking one's assumptions to scrutiny, one might fail to discover that one's understanding of the truth may be lopsided or incomplete.

Some virtues for integration focus on the character of the individual learner. Students must have an *honesty* that resists claiming as fact what is only comfortable or convenient. To enter into the integrative process, students need to be *self-possessed*. This means they know who they are and what they bring as strengths and limitations to the learning encounter. This quality of character emerges to the degree that an individual is *self-reflective* and can engage in metacognition to think about how one thinks. Learning in general and integration of learning in particular require a *capacity for change*. There are anecdotes about contemporary students for whom seminary formation or graduate study is an exercise in confirming what they already believe. The problem is not that someone has prior knowledge and belief when he or she enters a program of study and formation. In fact, such prior knowledge is an important bridge to new learning. But if what one knows to be true becomes the sole criterion by which all else is judged, a person seals herself or himself off from ways of seeing that can deepen and enrich how one sees the world and its meaning.

In a related way, integration requires of students a *tolerance for complexity*. The "simple beauty" of theology rests on a long history of thought, study, argument, missteps, and brilliant breakthroughs in the quest for a right understanding of God's revelation in Jesus Christ. That process never ends as each generation continues the task to know God truly in the context and circumstances of the age.

One insight from the Saint Meinrad's faculty is particularly enlightening as we consider student virtues or dispositions for integration. The faculty called this the virtue of *selflessness* in contrast to self-absorption. In all the classical descriptions of enlightenment, whether religious or intellectual, individuals who prosper are those whose pursuit of truth is not centered in themselves. That is, the discomfort in examining one's assumptions or the fear of considering a perspective that does not have the same contours as one's own view of the world or the simple hard work of seeing an argument that does not yield to easy analysis—none of these distract a person from engaging in a process of deep learning. It is a form of altruism because the end lies outside of one's immediate self-interest.

Cultivating these dispositions are important for helping students move more intentionally toward integration and for accepting the accountability implicit in them. It is equally important that students understand the structures that hold together a program of study. Students know how to go class, how to pray, and how to engage in field activities. Few students recognize that these discrete activities have a purposeful connection. Why should they? Undergraduate education has increasingly become compartmentalized and market-driven. There is no model upon which entering students can draw to engage graduate theological studies and formation as something in which the parts mesh. This lacuna means, then, that the orientation to the curriculum, advising, and other support services needs to introduce students to the complexities of a world of learning that has clear and integrative purposes.

Students may resist such an orientation either finding it demeans their capabilities or feeling it is something they should be able to catch onto as they proceed through the program. The latter may happen, but too many graduates of seminaries and schools of theology complete their programs in isolated units of class, chapel, field site, and counseling office. Institutions can likely not overdo describing the formative character of structures and programs, illustrating how the linkages among the parts occur, and how such linkages are sources of learning.

Integration as a Developmental Reality

In these final pages we return to one of the core attributes of integration—its developmental nature. People would likely agree that individuals do not either "get" integration or fail to do so. Anecdotal stories alone would indicate that individuals experience seeing-the-whole-for-the-parts at different points in their educational careers. For some it happens several years or more after graduation. One helpful model for this developmental approach is found in the work of Wiggins and McTigue.[9] They focus on a careful analysis of what it means to understand. Like integration, understanding is not an either/or proposition but a multifaceted phenomenon that unfolds over time and moves from less complex to more complex expressions.

Wiggins and McTigue argue that while everyone has a sense of what understanding means, a study of its facets or aspects enables one to *see* its complexity in a way that aligns with how one might develop competence in any one of the aspects. They identify six pivotal aspects of understanding: explanation, interpretation, application, perspective, empathy, and self-knowledge. For each aspect, they delineate performance levels that build on preceding capacities and extend the range of an individual's ability. The resulting matrix (see Figure 1 on pages 70–71) provides a map for developing pedagogical strategies that target ways for students to achieve greater sophistication in each aspect of understanding—in short, moving up the "developmental ladder." As an advising tool, the matrix enriches the counsel an adviser can offer a student. General exhortations to be better at interpreting the meaning of texts, for instance, gain specificity as the adviser helps a student gain insight into how what she does falls into an *interpreted stage* of development and what specific, concrete steps she will need to take to be able to do interpretation at *perceptive* or *revealing* levels.

The Wiggins-McTigue matrix offers a model for how a theological faculty might visualize its understanding of the integrative process. Visualization can move the intuitive judgments of faculty toward greater specificity. For the sake of an example, a faculty might determine that integration of master of divinity studies focuses on six key areas of pastoral leadership: preaching, worship, teaching, pastoral care, administration, and public service (see Figure 2 on page 72). As a group the faculty also agree that members will use four general stages of development applicable for each area: entry or novice, skilled, proficient, and advanced. These stages are not rigid but provide a general shared understanding for faculty *and for students* about what type of proficiency students should be able to demonstrate. The faculty may choose not to link each stage to a year of master of divinity studies while agreeing that students cannot be awarded a degree if they are not substantially able to demonstrate proficiency.

Furthermore, the description of each stage will include the mastery of knowledge, the demonstration of skills, personal insight and growth, and spiritual development. With this template in hand, the faculty sets about the demanding task of what faculty members will look for as students enter and progress through the master of divinity program. It is an invaluable task for it draws out faculty experience with diverse groups of learners over time and enriches the process of determining what characteristics are most reflective of a particular stage of development. At some point, the process will require a thorough examination of how the curriculum as a whole and each discipline, course, and formation requirement contributes to student integration.

The Saint Paul Seminary, for instance, has identified thirteen characteristics associated with human formation. A sample of stages of development is illustrated in Figure 3 on pages 72–73. The "stages" for the characteristics provide students time (keyed to year in formation), counsel, and experience as they move along this path toward integration.

Students need not wonder what faculty are looking for, and faculty members have a clear, specific way of sorting and assessing their experience with students as they advise them or recommend their advancement in the program. Equally important, by visualizing developmental expectations in this way, the faculty can more readily consider how courses within the curriculum relate to aspects of integration and how those courses need to be designed, taught, and interrelated so that students are encouraged to greater integration of the program in relation to pastoral leadership.

This exercise is labor intensive. It calls for a level of conversation that sets aside arguments about how much Scripture a student should have or whether twelve required credits in liturgical theology are too little or too much. Unpacking what comprises an "integrated graduate" requires making the implicit (that is, personal convictions and hunches of the faculty) explicit and discovering the wide range of opinion that exists. The investment in this process, however, results in a product that is far more precise and helpful for all those involved. The curriculum becomes an expression of what a faculty knows about student learning and formational development. It fosters agreement about how synergy of faculty effort creates a learning environment that is transparent in its expectations and purposefully supportive in the guidance it gives. Students are less focused on accumulating credits and more committed to engaging in activities of study, formation, and fieldwork as integral and interdependent dimensions of their self-understanding as pastoral ministers.

Conclusion

Approaching integration from a developmental perspective brings clarity to both understanding what it is and putting in place structures that facilitate its achievement. As will become evident in the next chapter, the intense amount of work this entails benefits the task of assessment that has gained urgency in higher education at all levels and for all professions. If the assessment question centers on validating what a faculty is seeking to accomplish, then the tasks of defining and clarifying the integrative outcomes of a formative program of study significantly facilitate the work of assessment.

The process sketched out above helps faculties be a bit more modest about what they can accomplish (or command be accomplished) and more realistic about what it takes to meet standards and expectations. Even if a faculty in the end chooses not to develop a formal developmental matrix regarding integration, discussion around the exercise itself insures that implicit assumptions buried in expectations become explicit. This step is important if students are to feel they are not victims of individual interpretation of standards or need to guess at what it takes to demonstrate increasing competence.

Competence as a professional pastoral minister underlies this exploration of integration. It may be nice for individuals to feel they have done more than accumulate credits, pass faculty scrutiny, and meet program expectations. Competence in the church's ministers, ordained or lay, however, is critical if the Gospel is to be preached boldly and if people are to find in their parishes a place that informs, forms, and directs their development as adult believers. While professional ministers certainly continue to grow and develop as they enter fulltime service, they build on a well-laid foundation in which intellectual, spiritual, pastoral, and human development continue to transform experience into meaning.

Integration within a Parish Context

While this reflection on integration focuses on graduate theological education, it offers some interesting questions and processes for consideration by parish pastoral leadership. All organizations risk fragmentation. It emerges as institutional leaders cope with the escalating demands of constituents, the scarcity of resources, the pressure of external forces, and the sheer weariness that can afflict even the most talented leaders.

Attention to integration as "seeing things whole" can be a way for parishes and their leadership to take stock of their commitments and to steward their resources in service of more than full service programming.

The following questions can encourage the sort of conversation among staff members and lay leaders that moves toward an "integrative appraisal" of parish life and ministries.

- **Staff focus**
  - What is the shared understanding among staff and lay leaders of the attributes of a "good parish"?
  - What is the shared understanding about the attributes that distinguish a "well-formed parishioner"? What does she or he look like?
  - To what extent does the parish mission statement offer an integrative focus for the work plan of the staff?
  - How do the dimensions of intellectual, pastoral, spiritual, and human formation affect the way parish leadership works with and engages adult members?
  - What specific, identifiable ways do staff members contribute to a common formation ethos in the parish?
  - How does the staff determine whether they are forming adults to be adult Catholics?
  - Can the staff describe the "developmental process" as a person moves toward being a well-formed parishioner?
  - Do staff members hold each other accountable for modeling the way well-formed parishioners live and act?

- **Parishioner focus**
  - What level of commitment does the parish have to insure that the professional ministry staff have the time, resources, and encouragement to pursue ongoing formation as individuals and especially as a team?
  - What are the practices and processes staff know work best in assisting adult members to develop integratively as members of a community of faith?
  - What virtues or dispositions do adult parishioners need to acquire and cultivate if they are to fulfill their responsibilities to grow as members of a faith community?

Figure 1
Wiggins and McTigue's Aspects of Understanding

EXPLANATION:	INTERPRETATION:	APPLICATION:
Why is it so? What explains such events? What accounts for such action? How can we prove it? To what is this connected? What is implied?	*What does it mean? Why does it matter? What does it illustrate or illuminate in human experience? What makes sense?*	*How and where can we use this knowledge, skill, or process? How should my thinking and action be modified to meet the demands of this situation?*
SOPHISTICATED: Unusually thorough sophisticated, elegant, and inventive account; fully verified and justified; deep and broad, going beyond the information given.	PROFOUND: Powerful and illuminating interpretation and analysis; tells a rich and insightful story; provides a rich history or context; sees deeply and incisively into different interpretations.	MASTERFUL: Fluent, flexible, and efficient; able to use knowledge and skill and adjust understandings well in novel, diverse, and difficult contexts.
IN-DEPTH: Atypical and revealing account, going beyond the obvious/what was explicitly taught; makes subtle connections; well supported by argument and evidence; displays novel thinking.	REVEALING: Nuanced interpretation and analysis; tells an insightful story; provides a telling history or context; sees subtle differences, levels, ironies in diverse interpretations.	SKILLED: Competent in using knowledge and skill and adapting understandings in a variety of appropriate and demanding contexts.
DEVELOPED: Account reflects some in-depth and personalized ideas; makes work one's own, going beyond the given. A theory offered but with insufficient or inadequate support.	PERCEPTIVE: Helpful interpretation or analysis; tells a clear and instructive story; provides a useful history or context; sees different levels of interpretation.	ABLE: Can perform well with knowledge and skill in a few key contexts, with a limited repertoire, flexibility, or adaptability to diverse contexts.
INTUITIVE: Incomplete account but with apt and insightful ideas; extends and deepens some of what was learned; some "reading between the lines"; account has limited support, argument or data or has sweeping generalizations. A theory offered but with limited testing, evidence.	INTERPRETED: Plausible interpretation or analysis; makes sense of a story; provides a history or context.	APPRENTICE: Relies on a limited repertoire of routines; can perform well in familiar or simple contexts, with perhaps coaching; limited use of personal judgment and responsiveness to specifics of feed-back or situation.
NAÏVE: Superficial account; more descriptive than analytical or creative; a sketchy description of facts/ideas or glib generalizations; a black-and-white account; less a theory than an unexamined hunch or borrowed idea.	LITERAL: Simplistic or superficial reading; mechanical translation; a decoding with little or no interpretation; no sense of wider importance or significance; a restatement of what was taught or read.	NOVICE: Can perform only with coaching or relies on highly scripted, singular "plug-in" skills, procedures, approaches.

PERSPECTIVE:	EMPATHY:	SELF-KNOWLEDGE:
From whose point of view or which vantage point? What is assumed and needs to be made explicit and considered? Adequate evidence? Plausible? Limits?	*How does it seem to you? What do they see that I don't? What do I need to experience if I am to understand?*	*How does who I am shape my views? What are limits to my understanding? My blind spots? What might I misunderstand because of habit, prejudice, or style?*
INSIGHTFUL: Penetrating and novel viewpoint; effectively critiques and encompasses other plausible perspectives; takes a long and dispassionate critical view of the issues involved.	MATURE: Disposed and able to see and feel what others see and feel; unusually open to and willing to seeking out the odd, alien, or different.	WISE: Deeply aware of the boundaries of one's own and others' understanding; able to recognize one's own prejudices and projections; has integrity—able and willing to act on what one understands.
THOROUGH: Revealing and coordinated critical view; makes own view more credible by considering the plausibility of other perspectives; makes apt criticisms, discriminations, and qualifications.	SENSITIVE: Disposed to see and feel what others see and feel; open to the unfamiliar or different.	CIRCUMSPECT: Aware of one's own ignorance and that of others; aware of one's prejudices; knows the strengths and limits of one's understanding.
CONSIDERED: Reasonable critical and comprehensive look at all points of view in the context of one's own; makes clear that there is plausibility to other points of view.	AWARE: Knows and feels that others see and feel differently; somewhat able to empathize with others; has difficulty making sense of odd or alien views.	THOUGHTFUL: Generally aware of what is and is not understood; aware of how prejudice can occur without awareness and shape one's views.
AWARE: Knows of different points of view and somewhat able to place own view in perspective; weakness in critiquing each perspective—especially one's own; uncritical about tacit assumptions.	DEVELOPING: Has some capacity and self-discipline to "walk in another's shoes" but is still primarily limited to one's own reactions and attitudes; puzzled or put off by different feelings or attitudes.	UNREFLECTIVE: Generally unaware of one's specific ignorance; generally unaware of how subjective prejudgments color understandings.
UNCRITICAL: Unaware of differing points of view; prone to overlook or ignore other perspectives; has difficulty imagining other ways of seeing things; prone to egocentric argument and personal criticism.	EGOCENTRIC: Has little or no empathy beyond intellectual awareness of others; sees things through own ideas and feelings; ignores or is threatened or puzzled by different feelings, attitudes, or views.	INNOCENT: Completely unaware of the bounds of one's understanding and of the role of projection and prejudice in opinions and attempts to understand.

Figure 2

A Developmental Framework for
Integration in the Master of Divinity Degree

Leadership Function \ Stage	ENTRY	SKILLED	PROFICIENT	ADVANCED
PREACHING				
WORSHIP				
TEACHING				
PASTORAL CARE				
ADMINISTRATION				
PUBLIC LEADERSHIP				

Figure 3

Characteristics of Development in Human Formation

Focus: In order that his ministry may be as humanly credible and acceptable as possible, it is important that the priest should mold his human personality in such a way that it becomes a bridge and not an obstacle for others in their meeting with Jesus Christ (*PDV*, 43).

STAGE I:

1. Manifests balance in the demands of study, prayer, service, and recreation by meeting his commitments in a timely fashion.
2. Exhibits openness and honesty in one-to-one conversations and in group settings.
3. Participates in group tasks in a collaborative spirit.

STAGE I–II:

4. Establishes and sustains friendships in which he deals appropriately with issues of intimacy and respects boundaries.
5. Engages positively in the formation program.
6. Shows respect and care for his body.
7. Relates socially with others by manifesting self-confidence, an interest in and concern for others, and an ability to put others at ease.

Figure 3 Continued

STAGE II:
8. Works effectively with people who are different than he is in race, sex, economic class, ethnicity, personality, ideology, role in the church.
9. Shows leadership ability in the seminary community and supervised ministry placements.
STAGE III–IV:
10. Shows consistency in the prudence and good sense of his judgments.
11. Manifests freedom from individualism.
12. Manifests compassion and generously assists others in need, particularly the poor and the disadvantaged.
13. Manifests a collaborative approach to ministry by trusting others, being sensitive to their needs and aspirations, using conflict constructively, and developing effective conflict resolution skills.

NOTES

1. Patricia Cranton, "Teaching for Transformation," *Contemporary Viewpoints on Teaching Adults Effectively,* Jovita M. Ross-Gordon, ed. *New Directions for Adult and Continuing Education* (Spring 2002) (San Francisco: Jossey-Bass, 2002) 63–64.

2. *The Basic Plan for the Ongoing Formation of Priests: A Statement of the U.S. Catholic Bishops* (Washington, D.C.: United States Catholic Conference, 2001) 8.

3. Part of unpublished work for a conference on the Character and Assessment of Religious Vocation sponsored by the Association of Theological Schools in Pittsburgh, November 2003.

4. The volume of literature on adult learning and learning in higher education has grown significantly in the past twenty years. One of the most helpful resources with excellent bibliographies is the series published by Jossey-Bass, *New Directions for Adult and Continuing Education.*

5. K. Patricia Cross and Mimi Harris Steadman, *Classroom Research: Implementing the Scholarship of Teaching* (San Francisco: Jossey-Bass, 1996). The "One Minute Paper" is adapted from this book.

6. William Bridges, *Transitions: Making Sense of Life's Changes,* 2nd ed. (Cambridge, Mass.: Perseus Publishing, 1980).

7. Unpublished conference notes.

8. From a faculty workshop held in September, 2003.

9. Grant Wiggins and Jay McTigue, *Understanding by Design* (Washington, D.C.: Association for Supervision and Curriculum Development, 1998).

CHAPTER 4

Assessment and Good Teaching

Over the past ten years, regional accrediting bodies and the Association of Theological Schools (ATS) escalated their emphasis on outcomes assessment. Those agencies began to ask schools for more explicit evidence that what they promised in catalogues actually happened. Because assessment was so often equated solely with statistical measurement of results, or worse, with a veiled attempt to discover failure, schools tended to regard it as a threat rather than as a resource.

At the same time, assessment in theological schools and seminaries had already been going on in other ways as schools pondered whether what they were doing was having the results they intended. The models of formation developed and refined the previous twenty-five years did not as readily produce a graduate who seemed prepared for the complexities of contemporary ministry. Nor did seminary students themselves show much eagerness for embracing programs and processes crafted by faculties to equip them for the ministry. The concern heightened as faculty began to notice changes in entering students' readiness for graduate study and professional formation described elsewhere in this book. Interestingly, while faculty often noted such global changes, they seemed inattentive to what was happening to the students in front of them who progressed through a system designed for a different type of student. "If we could just change the students by raising entrance requirements," tended to be the common response rather than, "What do we need to do differently in order to reach these new types of learners?"

Assessment helped sharpen the attention of theological schools and seminaries to this latter question despite legitimate complaints about some of the annoying aspects of the assessment movement in its early stages. When it is done well, assessment encourages renewed effort to listen more carefully to all participants in the preparation of students—including students themselves, experienced pastoral leaders, bishops, religious superiors, and the laity who are most directly affected by seminary graduates.

While there is in fact an evaluative aspect in assessment, it offers far more than that. Done well, assessment can contribute to the vitality of an educational institution, enrich the communal character of faculty life, engage students at a new level of responsibility, and cultivate a partnership with the local church that fosters mutuality, not struggle for control.

This chapter has three purposes. First, it makes the case for assessment as an educational practice that flows from the core concerns of seminaries and theological schools. Second, it describes practices that enable assessment to be a resource for achieving the quality everyone wants from an educational and formational program. Finally, the chapter concludes with comments about building a "culture for assessment" so that it becomes a normative practice in how a school goes about the work of education and formation.

The Case for Assessment: Servant vs. Master

In a thoughtful appraisal of the use of technology in theological education, Elizabeth Patterson observed that technology is a wonderful servant but a terrible master.[1] Her point was that what was intended as a tool for skilled teachers could too easily become like the school teacher in a Dickens novel—a master setting a beat with a switch to which all the students danced. Many faculty members would find Patterson's concern readily applicable to assessment. Because in its first iterations assessment was too often the "answer" to what ailed higher education, it became a bandwagon running on its own steam toward its own narrow ends. As a result, the purpose seemed to be some sort of forced conformity rather than a means to help faculties be more successful in their work of creating good theological schools.

There is an exercise that underscores the role of faculty members as masters of the assessment process rather than its servants. Faculty members first identify all the positive things for which their graduates are known. When that list is complete, they then name the gaps in the preparation of their graduates that various outside constituents most often mention. With those two sets of "data," the faculty can then explore two important assessment questions: How do they know these things are true, and who helps them recognize them? The simplicity of the exercise should not be misleading. A faculty knows a great deal about its graduates. In a very true sense, faculty members are the local experts about theological education, and that expertise is a starting point for productive assessment. This does not mean that there are no data to collect, surveys to write, and focus groups to lead. But methods to enrich the data come second. First of all, faculty need to recall that they begin the assessment process as people who observe, think about, draw conclusions, and explain what is going on in their classrooms and among students in their schools. John Harris and Dennis Sansom capture this well:

> The discernment needed to improve student learning does not lie primarily in finding ever more clever ways to measure students as determined organisms. Instead, the more productive approach lies in encouraging faculties to form communities of judgment to use the hard data and intuitive knowledge now available to them.[2]

Notice, however, that while Harris and Sansom urge faculties to draw on what they know, they do not stop there. Their concern for "hard data" picks up important questions in the exercise noted above: How do we know the conclusions drawn are valid and *who else can help verify them?* Much of what faculty members know can be accurate, but a portion is woven from sparse though often repeated anecdotes or generalizations about a handful of graduates. It is an understandably difficult task to stand outside of what one does as a pure objective observer. *Hard data* become a way to see objectively and to test conclusions for accuracy and lack of bias.

The question, "How do we know?" introduces discipline into how seminaries and schools of theology collect and interpret data. It is a question that deepens and expands the professional judgment of faculty members. Assessment is part of what a faculty does, and when the faculty fails to be the master of assessment, it risks gathering information that (1) can cause a momentary stir of interest that fades into business-as-usual, (2) can provoke a reflexive response that may or may not address the real issues being raised, or (3) can be accurate but lacks anyone willing to explore its meaning.

Six Principles about Assessment

Assessment has a growing body of literature that anchors it as a discipline and as an area of scholarly reflection.[3] At the same time, it also responds to the unique characteristics that define different areas of educational life. Six principles about assessment emerged as a result of the work of theological educators at the Keystone Conferences.

PRINCIPLE 1. *Assessment is native to what a faculty does.*

As intellectuals and scholars, faculty members ask questions, unpack assumptions, and examine phenomena from a variety of angles. In short, they are curious. Curiosity in this context is a spirit of inquisitive discontent to take something at face value. Assessment questions of a curious scholar might include:

- What is it we do to achieve the results to which we aspire?

- What pedagogical methods work? when? for what learning tasks? with whom?

- What formational practices draw the student into deep learning? What practices alienate the student? Why?

- How does the sequence of courses bear fruit? Does sequence matter? What are the key variables in sequencing that produce the results we seek?

An illustration of how a sense of curiosity can work involves a professor who taught the Hebrew Scriptures in a seminary for years. Father Smith was Roman-trained and employed a method used for eons: he lectured and students listened without showing much interest except in passing exams and producing a twenty-page research paper. Father Smith showed little initial interest when his dean provided in-service sessions on the changing needs of new learners, the use of technology as a teaching tool, and adult pedagogy. One day, however, he went into the office of the school's educational technologist and asked, "How can I help my students love the Old Testament as much as I do?" He began slowly, creating an active learning environment using Internet communication that transformed the learning experience of students. Some might say Father Smith acted out of desperation. An alternative view is that as he listened to his colleagues talk about teaching that encouraged active learning, his curiosity lead him to wonder about whether what he was doing to achieve his deepest purpose—to cultivate a love of his field—was in fact doing just the opposite.

If there is no curiosity about classroom pedagogy, the impact of courses, program expectations, and the environmental structures on learners, data collection becomes tedious, deadly, and useless. Avoid discussions of assessment that only involve counting noses—for example, how many people liked or disliked a team teaching approach? Let those discussions follow questions of curiosity. How do lectures stimulate active learning by students? What are habits, interactions, and teaching practices that create an environment where people achieve deep learning? Are students developing higher order skills that they will need to develop as good theologically-equipped pastors? How do students understand the connection between theory and praxis? Can students articulate what they think and believe regarding Scripture, values, mission, leadership, and the church?

PRINCIPLE 2. *Assessment is anchored in local expertise and the development of shared meaning within the faculty.*

One reaction to the overly mechanical approach in early outcomes assessment was the loss of confidence by faculty in their ability as a "community of judgment." The idea of "local expertise" focuses on the role faculty members have for tailoring assessment to the unique culture, mission, goals, norms, and wisdom of a given school. Models and examples of good assessment practice cannot function as templates that can be superimposed over any school to produce the information it needs.

Local expertise falters when a faculty neglects the hard work of achieving shared meaning about the key outcomes important to the success of the institution. Individual faculty members will of course assert what it means to be a good pastor or a good religious educator or liturgist. At the same time, those individual perspectives need to be refined in the forge of collegial discussion to yield a consensus about what this particular faculty of teachers agrees are the defining qualities of a graduate. That is a critical first step too often skipped over. It is tempting to say, "We all know what a good graduate looks like, don't we?" Heads bob because it seems true and because questioning that conclusion might lead to conflict and disagreement. It is better to let conflict serve as a refiner's fire at the consensus stage than to wait for it to erupt destructively later on. Once a faculty knows the qualities it seeks to foster, individual teachers then become accountable in a new way to their colleagues for the design and process of their courses.

Assessment done well moves a faculty from classroom autonomy to curricular interdependence. Professors no longer teach "their courses" but teach courses in the curriculum on behalf of the faculty *for the sake of learning*. No one is arguing to second guess a scholar's expertise in her discipline. If assessment is, however, about insuring that the curriculum coheres in its efforts to reach certain specific outcomes, individuals cannot choose to teach as though outcomes can be addressed selectively or ignored. The more interconnections that can be made between courses, the more likely it is for students to recognize and act upon them. Being intentional about connectedness does not enforce some sort of pedagogical uniformity on faculty. Rather, an awareness of what each other is doing and an openness to what needs to happen to advance the curriculum, cumulatively builds and deepens student ability and knowledge.

PRINCIPLE 3. *Assessment is more about a formative process than a summative product.*

Assessment as a formative process entails a commitment to make assessment a part of the regular work of the faculty. Collecting data for a decennial reaccreditation report may provide a helpful summative overview, but it is secondary to the formative impact of paying attention and responding to changing circumstances and emerging insights when assessment becomes mainstreamed. Focusing on the process of assessment rather than on its resulting data is a way of becoming a learning community around educational and formational issues in which reflection on practice breaks open new insight into the dynamics of effective teaching and learning.

PRINCIPLE 4. *Assessment is often a disruptive force in institutional life.*

Reframing assessment as an essential educational practice needs to acknowledge the costs involved. Perhaps the sharpest cost is the disruption that can occur when a faculty takes assessment seriously. What happens when the faculty pays attention to the gaps in the preparation of graduates for ministry? What changes need to occur when one's preferred style of teaching does not work with certain groups of learners? What rethinking follows the realization that students in an integrative seminar cannot integrate three or four years of classroom and fieldwork? How will a school respond when it discovers that graduates cannot do the work for parish ministry—or only with careful supervision?

While creating a "community of judgment" about assessment is in part a scholarly effort, the effort also means the disruption of routines, challenge to preferences and assumptions about what constitutes effective learning, and increased practice of teaching in public. These disruptions are in tension with an image of a seminary as a place of discourse around a curriculum so wise in its construction it seldom needs tending and with a body of learners homogenous in their preparation and disciplined in their readiness to sit at the feet of Wisdom. Assessment is an explicit acknowledgment that curricula are vessels of clay that need frequent remolding in order to hold water; that the work of ministry formation is as complex and demanding as the ministries into which graduates will move; that students come into the process at a hundred different starting points with a readiness that is rich, diverse, and often incomplete all at the same time. The resulting disruption need not be chaotic, but it requires a flexibility and an alertness that can be wearying.

PRINCIPLE 5. *Assessment is the work of the faculty.*

There is a temptation to shift the work of assessment to the dean, an assessment officer, or an assessment committee—all of whom have roles to play in the process. Their work, however, is dependent on the faculty's articulated need for information that can best assist them in their work as teachers. If faculty members are not asking questions, identifying appropriate sources of evidence, and interpreting results, assessment falters. A faculty enjoys authority because of the expertise of its members. Their authority also rests on the fact that they are self-critical and able to receive feedback from others as they tend to what helps the school meet its stated purposes.

Assessment is not a mathematical puzzle that proves a faculty is good. Rather, it offers insight that enables faculty members to do what they have to do to (1) invite learners to see the beauty of the truth they see, (2) equip them with the knowledge, skills, and dispositions for pastoral leadership, and (3) instill in them the disciplines needed to carry forth the enduring traditions of the church. Others will legitimately have additional expectations, but those expectations should themselves be subject to the faculty's assessment scrutiny.

PRINCIPLE 6. *Assessment has its greatest impact when there is alignment of effort throughout the institution.*

Alignment of goals insures that individual courses and formation requirements form a coherent program of study that expresses the institution's public mission. Assessment as an educational practice helps identify how intellectual, pastoral, spiritual, and human formation mutually contribute to the overall purposes of a school, and how leveraging what each area does can in fact maximize what the curriculum can accomplish. Achieving balance and rhythm in a curriculum requires making choices. Unless there is an alignment of goals at course, program, and institutional levels, those choices are generally governed by persons with the loudest voices or the ability to muster the greatest pressure.

Alignment also helps constituents better understand what is at stake in the design of educational and formation programs. This may have particular significance as the seminary and local church discuss what ministerial formation should entail. The clarity that alignment of goals requires can serve as a common point of dialogue in which the integral nature of formation is viewed as a whole rather than as an entity with interchangeable parts.

Practices that Cultivate Assessment as an Educational Resource

Excellent resources are available to guide faculties as they begin to build a "culture of evidence" in their institutions.[4] The following practices primarily aim at issues of clarity and alignment as a faculty develops its expertise at assessing its work and its impact on learning and formation.

Practice I: Achieving Consensus

This exercise guides faculty members in clarifying program outcomes as a means of achieving consensus about what to assess. In a faculty of twenty members, there can be a wide, often unspoken range of perceptions about what aspects of program outcomes are most insightful in terms of knowledge, skills, and attitudes. Using the master of divinity degree as an example of how this exercise works, faculty members first individually reflect on the outcomes of the degree using Figure 1 as a guide. The three core characteristics reflect primary areas of concern for the ministry graduate: spiritual/human formation, academic competence, and pastoral development. For each core characteristic, the faculty member lists the attributes that provide indicators of achievement. Note that while all attributes need not be measured in quantitative terms, all need to be observable.

Figure 1

Achieving Consensus about Program Outcomes

Core Characteristics of the Master of Divinity Graduate			
	The Pastoral Minister as Person of Faith and Good Character	The Pastoral Minister as Lifelong Student of Christian Teaching	The Pastoral Minister as Leader in Church and Community
ATTRIBUTES Behaviors That We Can Observe, Measure, and/or Discern			

Once individuals have completed the handout, they form small groups and begin the challenging work of building consensus about which attributes best capture what the degree seeks to accomplish in terms of its core characteristics. This is not a simple exercise because it reveals fundamental assumptions people hold about the purposes of the master of divinity degree. The investment of time and energy demanded by this practice, however, helps surface program outcomes that are not well framed, are incomplete or redundant, or are *overstatements of what the institution has the capacity to accomplish.* This latter discovery can be emancipating for faculties who have struggled with institutional or program goals that, while excellent examples of compelling rhetoric, lack the precision needed for assessment. More importantly, such goals can ultimately fail to reflect what in fact the faculty does.

Practice II:
Identifying Appropriate and Effective Sources of Information

Once a faculty agrees on the attributes that best reflect program outcomes, members need to determine sources of information on those attributes that will provide meaningful feedback. Figure 2 provides a means to structure this practice for reflection and discussion and has two focal points: what sort of information will offer the most insightful and convincing evidence and what sources can generate that information. There is a temptation to accumulate "data" whose primary purpose is to meet constituent demands for accountability or to prove that the status quo is fulfilling program purposes. If assessment is to work, the sort of evidence generated must have persuasive value for those making program decisions. Faculty members need to ask themselves, then, "What information from which sources will be most useful as we consider the strengths and weaknesses of our formation programs, our teaching, and our curricula? What questions do we need to ask and who should be responding?" Surveys, focus groups, comprehensive exams, research theses, project reports, portfolios, reports from field supervisors, longitudinal studies, evaluations from first pastors and parishioners or diocesan personnel officers—all these can be good sources of data. The challenge is to know which will make the difference in how faculty or staff members reflect on what they are doing.

Practice III: Aligning Program and Mission Outcomes

Creating alignment of program outcomes with mission outcomes begins to build greater synergy among the efforts of the faculty. It is striking sometimes to discover that revisions of degree programs take little notice of the institution's mission or that the revision process is not an occasion to consider the adequacy of the mission of the seminary or theological school. In this exercise, the faculty regularly reviews degree program outcomes in light of institutional mission and purposes by placing degree outcomes next to institutional outcomes and then exploring the relationships that exist or do not exist. The process is another way of achieving clarity about what people think the stated outcomes of their institution mean and how they become embodied in the core work of the school. In most instances, some implicit link usually exists between institutional and program goals, but for some there may well be no apparent relationships. This scenario does not necessarily suggest misalignment, but it calls for deeper conversation about how programs manifest the mission of the school, and how the various programmatic efforts of a school work together to achieve the mission. Alignment helps alert faculty to barriers that can arise

Figure 2

Identifying Useful Assessment Information

Core Characteristic: *Minister as Person of Faith and Good Character*		
	BEST EVIDENCE	BEST SOURCE
Attribute I:		
Attribute II:		
Attribute III:		

between areas of a curriculum (for example, theological studies and field education), between disciplines within a curriculum, or between programs with distinctive outcomes (for example, master of divinity versus master of arts in theology). Being able to map the school's agenda facilitates the process of gathering and interpreting evidence about its effectiveness.

Practice IV: Aligning Course and Program Outcomes

A course functions at three intersecting levels. First, there is the integrity of the course content itself. A second level is how the course advances the outcomes of the degree program and the institution. While course content might stand alone, it takes on particular meaning within the framework of a program of studies and the purposes of the institution. Finally, a course strives to enable students to practice the abilities and skills needed to demonstrate proficiency regarding course content and to program and institutional outcomes. This complex set of intersections is one of the reasons faculty members groan over the work of assessment. While it is a challenge to engage students in a disciplined study of theology as an end in itself, considering the relationship between professional competence and program and institutional outcomes is not a matter of degree; it is a quantum shift in what needs to happen in the classroom.

Figure 3 is an example of how faculty members might "map" the alignment of what they do in their individual courses with the intended outcomes of the program and the school. The instructor need not

Figure 3

Aligning Course and Program/Institutional Outcomes

	Demonstrates How the Tradition Sheds Light on a Pastoral Situation	Shows Awarenes of Own Strengths and Weaknesses	Organizes Material Logically in Written and Oral Forms	Shows Capacity for Effecitve Preaching
Course Outcome and/or Course Expectation I				
Course Outcome and/or Course Expectation II				
Course Outcome and/or Course Expectation III				

abandon her or his commitments to scholarly content. Rather, the challenge is to be more explicit and intentional in helping students see how a particular course fits into and supports a network of purposeful outcomes. For faculty this network may be obvious. For a substantial portion of students, it is not. Faculty complaints about students coming to dogmatic courses ill-equipped in Scripture *after* completing three Scripture courses are echoed by liturgical theology faculty who discover that students with six graduate credits of study in church history lack any sense of historical method. The exercise in Figure 3 helps individual faculty members become more conscious about how the courses they teach help convey the core commitments of the school and its programs.

The process of alignment encourages an instructor to identify explicitly how a current outcome or activity relates to course purposes as well as to program and institutional outcomes. It can also reveal that an instructor might need to develop ways in which to make those relationships clearer.

This process cuts close to the bone regarding instructor autonomy. Not only does it make the work in the classroom more public; it also begins to hold individual instructors accountable in a way that is often new and sometimes awkward. At the same time, the conversation prompted by the process can surface significant pedagogical creativity and versatility already present in the faculty. As faculty explore what they do to advance the outcomes of the program and institution or solicit advice from colleagues on what they might do, the formation of a community of teachers begins to emerge. This formation is good not only for the enrichment of pedagogy; it also creates new ferment about the ways in which assessment can be directly useful to faculty at the course level.

Building a Culture for Assessment

Training specialists in business and industry argue that innovation in companies depends on ongoing training. As obvious as it might seem, the addition of assessment to the agenda of faculties was doomed to resistance because often it was perceived as foreign matter and introduced without any sort of training program in place. Assessment is indeed a core part of educational practice. Its ascendance to new prominence with its own disciplinary character has taken place haphazardly at best. Two factors are instrumental in changing a disposition about assessment characterized by distrust, suspicion, and loathing. One is cultivating the expertise of faculty as teachers, and the other relates to having a plan for assessment grounded in a compelling rationale for why we engage in assessment.

A Community of Teachers

Forming a community of teachers demands time and courage. We have learned from our experience at the Keystone Conferences that no school has found a rhythm of life that leaves large chunks of time unspecified. The scramble to be "full service schools" no matter the size of the student body or faculty results in a perpetual sense of overload. Although faculty members might theoretically believe that talking about teaching would be useful, they usually shake their heads in dismay at adding "one more meeting." Talking about teaching is more than "one more meeting." It is key to institutional effectiveness and the place where assessment information has the greatest relevance. Administrators need to become far more able to create meaningful space for such conversations.

Becoming a community of teachers also takes courage for reasons alluded to earlier. Talking about teaching takes one from the surety of disciplinary mastery to the not-so-sure world of classroom instruction. Behind closed doors one might imitate practices of her or his best professors, might try new approaches to teaching, or might choose to exercise imperial rule over all who enter. The imperious are a minority. Far

more members of a faculty may feel like imposters—people who probably are the worst teachers in the school or certainly not as skilled as
Dr. Smith or Father Jones. Stephen Brookfield speaks frequently about
the "impostership syndrome" and indicates that the only remedy is to go
public.[5] By this he means engaging in the sort of collegial conversation
that helps individuals discover that almost every other member of the
faculty feels unskilled and unsuccessful at some time. "Teacher talk" is
not group therapy; it is professional development.

Classroom assessment practice draws directly on classroom experience and enables faculty members to build and enhance their roles as
local experts in their teaching fields. Classroom assessment achieved
prominence with the work of Patricia Cross and Thomas Angelo who
felt that teachers could equip themselves to learn from their teaching as
they teach.[6] End-of-term course evaluations have limited usefulness in
this regard. They provide anonymous assessments of students at a point
in the learning process in which the information given can contribute
nothing to learning. That a faculty person can use that data the next
time she or he teaches has some value, but not enough to make faculty
members local experts. Classroom assessment can.

Classroom assessment is a formative practice using a wide variety of
techniques to determine how students are learning. Under the control
of the instructor, the techniques provide efficient opportunities to assess
whether what one is presenting in a lecture, facilitating in a process, or
assigning in a bibliography is having its intended outcome. One example is known as the "Application Card." At the end of a session and
at a strategic point in the course, the instructor describes a pastoral
situation that would entail use of the materials presented, discussed,
and read. He or she gives students an index card and asks them to respond to the situation based on what they have learned in the course.
The instructor collects the cards and sorts them according to appropriate, inadequate, and simply wrong applications. At the start of the next
course session, the instructor summarizes applications that hit the mark
and where other applications need rethinking. There is still time to
guide students in becoming more skillful in making applications.

As faculty members use techniques like this as ways to pay attention
to learning as it unfolds, they become increasingly attuned to what
they do, to students' responses, and to ways to adjust, enrich, change,
or expand their approach to a topic to greater access for students. In addition, in a faculty where members regularly talk about teaching, what

people are learning from classroom assessment can enrich their help-fulness to one another.

Finally, the development of local expertise about classroom teaching bears directly on the way an institution does assessment. Attentive to the dynamics of learning at the local level of a classroom, faculty can begin to imagine what needs to happen at the more global level of the program. The sorts of questions they generate to assess the cumulative impact of institutional efforts are less random and speculative and more targeted on the link between specific institutional practices and its stated outcomes. Curiosity about one's teaching and the skill to pursue that curiosity through classroom teaching influences how one thinks about what the seminary or school of theology is doing.

Working from a Plan

Although assessment is a disposition towards learning and a prac-tice of asking questions stirred by one's curiosity, it also has component parts that form a plan. The components often remind the faculty of steps they need to take in order to transform unrefined data into a highly useful source of insight for doing well what it is the faculty want to achieve.[7]

1. *Develop a rationale statement that situates assessment within the culture and ethos of the school.*

Developing a rationale for the work of assessment articulates the faculty's understanding of assessment, the values with which it under-takes the work of assessment, and the general aims toward which the results are directed. Two benefits result from investing faculty time to construct a rationale. First, it puts the faculty's "thumbprint" on the process and shifts the focus from the mechanics of data gathering to congruence with mission. While acknowledging the sometimes formi-dable impact outside agencies can have on a school, the work of assess-ment itself is under the direction of the faculty. External expectations need to be "translated" so they are related to how a school understands itself. A second benefit of a well-developed rationale is that it provides a way to orient new faculty to the role of assessment and to provide a record as future faculty members pick up and extend assessment as an institutional resource.

2. *Identify program goals that reflect faculty members' convictions regarding what students should know, value, and be able to do.*

Theoretically, when faculty members identify a program outcome, they are asserting that they can determine and verify that the outcome is being achieved. The clarity with which the outcome is stated, therefore, is critical to an effective assessment plan.

Outcomes that relate to less tangible realities—growth as a person or a deeper relationship with God—should be framed in terms of specific attributes of knowledge, attitude, or behavior that faculty members have come to recognize as signs of goal attainment.

Outcomes of a program over which faculty members have little direct control should not be formulated as *assessment goals*. For example, a program can help students acquire an understanding of the history of Christian spirituality and the practice of spiritual disciplines common to the tradition. The faculty cannot determine whether the student loves God more deeply as a result.

Resist allowing rhetorical flourishes to override clarity of purpose. Clear goals enable effective assessment because they already state what faculty members have learned they can "see" in some way in a well-prepared graduate.

3. *Assessment procedures are appropriate for observing what each goal intends to accomplish.*

Surveys are useful instruments. They have no divine origin or endorsement. Sometimes surveys are the best way to ask important questions; at other times focus groups are indispensable. In some instances, the use of field supervision reports is key; at other times, assessment of students' preaching or final theses by an outside team offers insight no other method can accomplish. In short, not just any procedure will do but only those that are best suited to give insight into what a particular goal intends.

4. *Multiple assessment procedures get at different aspects of an intended outcome.*

Think of this component in these familiar terms. If an instructor wanted to know whether a student understood her class on the Gospel of John, she could construct an exam; have the student write an exegetical paper; have him do a class presentation on christology using John's Gospel; listen to him preach on a passage; or invite a colleague in New Testament studies to interview him on what he knows. Some of these methods assess for content mastery; others look at various applications; and the last has someone who knows the topic, but not the student, determine the level of his understanding. Having several procedures for an outcome broadens what one knows about the effects of teaching and student learning.

5. *Make the plan efficient so that it builds on activities already implemented that can become valuable sources of information related to program and institutional outcomes.*

Somewhere along the line the notion arose that a faculty needed to start from scratch as it developed its assessment plan. Part of being a community of judgment is that faculty members are already working with sources of information that form their judgments. Consider how those can continue to be used or refashioned in some way to be even more useful. What does the school already have in place in terms of relationships with various constituencies that might easily be adapted as sources of insight on assessing outcomes? Examples include periodically sampling master's theses or integration projects for intensive analysis rather than assessing every graduating student's work; or adding questions to annual alumni/ae surveys; or reviewing the structure and content of graduate exit interviews.

6. *Control for bias in gathering and interpreting assessment data by providing ways for people outside the faculty to assist in the process.*

Controlling bias might be a matter of inviting a small team of pastors to view and rate recorded student sermons using a set of criteria developed by the faculty. A team of qualified colleagues from outside the school could periodically read and assess a sample of research papers using a faculty-designed rating system. Recall the value of reports from field placement supervisors or the summary evaluations from clinical pastoral education. Supervisors might be even more helpful if they had a few key questions generated by the faculty to guide them.

7. Make the assessment plan explicit by writing it down.

In the end, this is a plan. Putting it in writing helps insure that everyone knows its parameters, expectations, emphases, and limitations. A written plan makes sure that there is leadership and that everyone understands the roles and responsibilities involved. It describes how data will be evaluated and acted on. In short, the plan becomes a guiding text and controls for the suspicion that assessment is ultimately about finding out "what we do wrong." Specialists in assessment theory and practice would argue that an assessment plan for a faculty is a statement of its research purposes: what do we want to know, how will we go about collecting information, and what will we do with what we learn? Unstated plans do not usually get far.

8. The assessment plan should be specific about addressing any areas for improvement identified in the assessment.

It is easy for assessment data to get lost amidst the busy demands of institutional life. The neglect is benign; it also wastes a great deal of good thinking and effort. In the written plan, there should be a sufficiently detailed procedure of how information learned will get into the faculty decision-making processes. Not every finding in assessment demands action or change. Faculty might discover that graduates question the value of having to complete twenty-one credits of Scripture study in a master of divinity degree. A faculty might consider that finding and decide that they will not change the requirement, but they might also consider ways to help students understand why the requirement is so steep in relationship to other areas of the curriculum. Responding to assessment outcomes is always important. A response, however, is not synonymous with making a change—today. The other benefit of closing the loop in assessment is that as faculty develop a pattern of reflecting on assessment data and using them to inform their deliberations and decisions, members begin to generate more precise, targeted questions. Good questions are critical to good assessment.

Conclusion

This chapter argues that assessment is a practice hospitable and integral to the work of a faculty. The effort to situate it in the unique setting and mission of each school and under the direction and control of the faculty is not an attempt to put a happy face on an unavoidable task imposed by forces outside the institution. Even without the expectations of professional and regional accrediting agencies, good theological schools would do assessment in some form because good schools are interested in knowing how they are doing. Good schools have a sense of accountability to their partners that include the students, sponsoring bishops and religious communities, and those congregations and institutions that will depend on the skillful leadership and talent of graduates. Arguing for assessment is arguing for the obvious: How do we establish ways to keep ourselves alert to changing contexts, changing learner needs, and changing expectations so that what we do educationally and formationally makes a purposeful difference—not by accident or by virtue of who participates but because of intentional, well-considered actions?

This is the reason why assessment needs to be anchored in a compelling rationale or vision, not just in a set of procedures or even in a plan. A vision for assessment can sustain and challenge a faculty in the face of temptations to be content with what exists. The collegial work of constructing a rationale takes faculty into some basic questions: What outcomes do we most want and/or need to explore? Which has the greatest priority for us? Why do we want to know about these outcomes? What are our criteria for judging success? What are the best sources of information? How will we use information we collect? These are practical questions, to be sure, but they hone a faculty's attentiveness. And in the act of being attentive to the confluence of actions and attitudes, strategies and resources, a faculty discovers how best to be a center of learning and formation for the church and the world to which it witnesses.

Assessment and the Parish

It is probably safe to assert that few parishes have an assessment plan. Parishes are often places where much of what goes on occurs as part of an oral culture in which past practices tend to lead present decisions. As Kathleen Cahalan argues in her recent book on evaluation in religious organization, the lack of good assessment or evaluation is not only deficient organizational practice, it can also lead to poor stewardship.[8] Parish staffs and lay leaders in the parish might reflect on how assessment can become a resource for effective pastoral mission by considering the components of an assessment plan.

- **Vision, goals, and strategies**
- What rationale or vision for assessment in the parish would help professional and lay leadership tailor assessment practices to the learning needs of the parish?

- Does the parish have clear, articulated goals that determine the best deployment of time, effort, and resources?

- What strategies for assessing parish goals would be most effective in providing the information that staff and lay leaders need to make decisions?

- **Perspectives and accountability**
- What are the various means that staff and lay leaders can use to provide a well-rounded understanding of activities and their impact?

- What is the parish already doing to assess program effectiveness and how can those efforts be strengthened and the information used more intentionally?

- How might the parish draw on outside perspectives to provide an objective view of programs and their contribution to advancing the mission of the parish?

- When an assessment plan is written down, who will be responsible for its implementation, review, and revision?

- How will the information generated by a planned process of assessment be used in making decisions about programs, new initiatives, and future planning?

NOTES

1. Elizabeth Patterson, "The Questions of Distance Education," *Theological Education* (1996) 59–74.

2. John Harris and Dennis Sansom, "Discerning Is More than Counting," Occasional Papers in Liberal Education, 3, *American Academy for Liberal Education* (2000) 20.

3. The work of Trudy Banta and her associates is particularly useful. See Trudy W. Banta, *Building a Scholarship of Assessment* (San Francisco: Jossey-Bass, 2002).

4. Carolyn Jurkowitz, "What Is the Literature Saying about Learning and Assessment in Higher Education?" *Theological Education* (2003) 53–93.

5. Stephen Brookfield, *The Skillful Teacher: On Technique, Trust and Responsiveness in the Classroom* (San Francisco: Jossey-Bass, 2000).

6. Thomas A. Angelo and K. Patricia Cross, *Classroom Assessment Techniques: A Handbook for College Teachers* (San Francisco: Jossey-Bass, 1993). The "Application Card" is adapted from the book.

7. Except for the first component, "Developing a Rationale," these features of a plan are adapted from material developed by Ball State University and presented at a conference of the American Association of Higher Education, June 2001.

8. Kathleen Cahalan, *Projects that Matter: Successful Planning and Evaluation in Religious Organizations* (Alban Institute, 2003).

CHAPTER 5

Building Communities of Wisdom

Introduction

In American culture we are often reminded of the "power of one." Linked to our heritage of rugged individualism, we frequently find ourselves underscoring the significance of the work of one person, like inventor Thomas Edison, civil rights leader Martin Luther King, Jr., political and religious leader Sojourner Truth, or successful business- man Bill Gates. All of these people reflect the "power of one" whose success in his or her particular area has had far reaching ramifications for the good of humanity.

As effective as the power of one is, imagine the "power of many." Consider the impact of the first disciples of Jesus, committed as they were to him and to his mission; the courage of the villagers of Le Chambon in France, responsible for saving the lives of countless Jews during the Second World War; or marchers for civil rights in the mid-1960s in this country. The power of the group goes beyond the simple assertion, "There is strength in numbers." Rather, to effect change there surely is eminently more wisdom, zeal, and energy in a group.

This chapter argues that the formation of the faculty as a community of wisdom is the vehicle for effective responses to the challenges raised in this volume. It develops further some of the principles offered in the chapter on the role of leadership within an institution. The material presented here, moreover, has applicability for any church group intent on tapping the riches of a diverse body of persons committed to a common purpose.

Why is communal faculty development of particular value and sig- nificance? Quite simply, the faculty is the core of any educational insti- tution. Administrators and students come and go, but rarely does an institution lose a significant number of faculty members at once. Consequently, the faculty is the body primarily responsible for achieving the mission, the principal bearer of institutional culture, and the group who must respond most directly to the challenges of theological and learning diversity, integration, and assessment.

Faculty members are in a unique position because of their day-to-day contact with students and administrators; they know what the institution says it is and what is, in fact, the reality. Well-written catalogues and carefully crafted accreditation reports aside, it rests with the faculty to keep the word of the institution and the promises it makes for the education of its students. In short, the faculty governs the whole educational process and deserves the investment of time, energy, and resources to equip it to work as a body in fulfilling all that is expected of it. Anything less is irresponsible.

In an ideal world, faculties would regularly participate in extended periods of communal rest and reflection on the issues they face. Such a notion is unrealistic given the pace and workload of most schools. Yet, faculties can set aside *sabbatical time* in other ways within the school year by structuring particular gatherings to focus intentionally on their deepest concerns and challenges as an institution. Such a strategy exceeds what can occur in monthly faculty meetings where agendas seem to get longer while the time to consider issues grows shorter. Creating a community of wisdom requires time and an atmosphere as in a sabbatical.

This chapter offers a blueprint for communal faculty development drawn from the Keystone Conferences' experience and concludes with words of advice from faculty members and administrators who participated in those events. The purpose is to share a proven model for developing faculties who are wise in the endeavors of theological education and adept at sharing their riches with others.

Building a Community of Wisdom:
Principles and Processes

The Keystone Conferences gathered faculty teams for a week of reflection, prayer, and relaxation at the center of which was a common concern for the quality and effectiveness of teaching and learning. Over the six years we learned a great deal about how to create an environment and frame tasks that would draw on the rich resources and experience of participants. The description of the principles that informed our design of the conferences and processes that facilitated their success illustrate key elements for communal faculty development.

Practice 1. Naming the Issue

A first step for faculty development is naming the issue. This begins by reflecting on the mission of the institution and raising issues that require attention for the effectiveness of the teaching and learning process.

Process for Naming the Issue

A helpful process for naming the issue from among all the possibilities is called "Simple Sharing, Corporate Listening." It is a simple yet very effective process.

Simple Sharing, Corporate Listening

Goal: To have the group identify the issue they want to focus on as a project of communal faculty development.

Process:

1. The leader of the group assigns a person to record the comments made by participants.

2. During the "simple sharing," the leader goes around the room and asks each person for input. For example, the leader inquires: "To what do we need to give our attention if we are to develop as a faculty? What issue merits extended reflection by us and our whole institution?" Everyone attending the meeting must speak. Participants may "pass" when it is their turn, but the leader comes back to them so that everyone expresses an opinion. During this phase of the process, participants are not to refer to what others have said, but merely state their own opinion.

3. Having heard from each participant at the meeting, the group begins the Corporate Listening phase. The leader might ask, "What did you hear?" "Was a common theme evident?" "Can we make any connections among the various issues that were raised?"

Outcome: The group comes to agreement on a faculty development issue.

It would be unrealistic to think that a process like simple "corporate listening" leads immediately to consensus among participants. It does, however, provide a means to hear all voices with their rationales. Having considered the input of all, the group must move to the selection of a particular issue that requires their attention.

Practice 2. Framing the Issue with a Case Study

Once the issue has been named and agreed upon by the faculty, it must be framed within the context of the particular institution. For example, a pastoral theology faculty member raises a question about what it means to teach with a pastoral perspective. She relates a recent conversation with a graduating student who told her that he can't wait to get out of the seminary and into the real world where he won't be caught up in studies, papers, and the rest of academic life. Acknowledging the student's legitimate desire to begin full-time ministry, the professor wonders whether the courses taught in the seminary provide students with theological knowledge but fail to build connections between theology and pastoral practice. In her experience, students seem to forget their theology when they enter pastoral situations, relying on some sort of "pastoral instinct" whether it is particularly sound theologically or not. Because this issue takes on heightened importance within an institution whose mission is to prepare people for ministry, it offers a tangible case that helps all parties see themselves in the situation and responsible for addressing the dilemma.

Process for Framing the Issue: Writing a Case Study

Although there are countless ways to tackle a problem in our day-to-day lives, case studies have proven to be very effective tools to analyze issues. In order to work well, they must be carefully composed. The reader should be caught up by the story and feel compelled to respond in some way to the dilemma posed. Case studies are narratives that present real characters in a real institution, even though names should be changed. The narrative does not exhaust all that can be said about a particular issue but merely offers a "snap shot" of the dilemma that participants can further investigate. It provides a "text" for discussion of the issue, engaging the various constituencies within the institution.

Elements of a Good Case Study

1. Describe the facts of a given situation in an engaging way.

2. Frame an issue in its complexity, attempting to get all the "players" into the case study in some way without providing an analysis.

3. Present the case study so that the reader sees himself or herself in the story with responsibility for decision making/action at some level.

Practice 3. Getting Everyone on Board

Successful faculty development must have broad support starting with the faculty and administrative leaders. It is also important that other constituents, like the board of trustees and students, are aware of the commitment of the faculty to its own development and its link to the overall mission of the school. Leaving principal people out of the loop undermines the formation of a wisdom community and impedes progress toward addressing the challenges and opportunities in an institution's life.

Fostering Broad Ownership

How might one go about "getting everyone on board"? Presuming that the critical issue surfaced has the support of all parties, leadership could present a draft of the case study to a group of representatives from all constituencies to test the adequacy of how the issue is framed.

Questions for Evaluating the Feasibility of the Case Study

1. Does this case study reflect the issue within our institutional context?

2. Is there anything or anyone missing from the case study that is essential to describing accurately the dilemma our institution or community faces?

3. Can we agree that this case study adequately describes the issue, and can we proceed with this case as our working text?

In the process of "getting on board," of course, it is not uncommon to encounter the resisters in the group. Vocal resisters can actually be quite helpful in a process of communal faculty development because they generally help the community to focus and to stay on track. Unless resisters simply argue for the sake of arguing, the group might find their questions and objections helpful in sharpening the rationale for both the choice of issue and the manner of presentation in the case study. As much as the resister can be a thorn in the group's side, it is always instructive to ask, "What can we learn from the questions being raised here? What wisdom resides in the voice of the resister?"

Practice 4. Engage the Case Study

Once the case study has framed and contextualized the issue, it is time to engage the case. A couple of points should be kept in mind to facilitate the successful discussion of the case and to establish an environment for focused work.

Steps toward Creating an Environment for Engaging the Case Study

Three factors will be helpful in working on a project and engaging the case study: a change of environment, outside facilitation, and working as a group with carefully designed processes.

Unquestionably, Keystone provided an idyllic atmosphere for relaxation, but it also served as a helpful place to work. To a person, the participants noted the advantage of being in a setting apart from their own institutions to dedicate time specifically to a particular issue of significance. Never underestimate the value of getting away to relax and to work collaboratively. Even a single overnight event that runs from noon to noon can foster a deeper sense of community that helps accent the group's common purpose.

A second factor that influences the success of case study discussions is the use of outside facilitators. Carefully chosen consultants bring fresh sets of eyes and experience to the institution. Faculties are often on their "best behavior" in the presence of outsiders, helping faculty members stay focused on the task and cooperate with one another in productive ways. It is important to remember that the consultant's value is not so much as an expert with all the answers, but as someone who elicits from the group the wisdom each member bears.

Finally, engaging a case study succeeds to the degree that it is the work of the group. Communal development of a faculty presumes working together whether in plenary session or in small groups. This means designing a process tailored to the culture and personality of the faculty or staff as a group that can tap the insight, wisdom, and experience of each member.

Process for Engaging the Case Study[1]

We are at the point when the group engages the narrative of the case study. In doing so, particular tasks need attention.

Become Familiar with the Substance of the Case
What is going on?
Is relevant information missing?
What are the facts as presented in the case?

Identify the Principal Issues
What decisions will have to be made in light of the case?
Who is going to be responsible for making these decisions?
Prior to making the decision, what other factors, issues, and
    consequences must be attended to?

Note Objectives and Goals to Be Achieved
What solutions to this issue are possible within our institution or
    community?
What outcomes would be desirable?
Who has a stake in the various outcomes and why?

Identify Resources and Obstacles
What facilitates or stands in the way of some of the proposed reso-
    lutions to the dilemma?
What resources can we draw upon to move ahead in this project?
What challenges will we face?

Consider the Nature of Conflicts that Might Arise
What conflicts might arise in the course of addressing this issue (i.e.,
    resistance)?
What precisely is at the heart of the conflict?
What is at stake?
How can conflicting positions and plans of action be reconciled?
Is an effective compromise workable?

Identify Dynamics of Behavior

Who seems to be exercising leadership in the case?

Where are interpersonal conflicts evident?

Imagine Viable Alternative Ways of Proceeding

How can we take advantage of the variety of perspectives in the room?

How can we encourage people to release their imaginations in considering alternative courses of action?

Evaluate Consequences of Proposed Decisions and Actions

What will result from particular decisions?

What unintended consequences might arise?

How can we deal with them?

Can we name the short-term and long-term consequences for both individuals and the institution as a whole?

Brainstorm Effective Strategies to Move Forward

What strategies can be employed to move toward action in addressing the issue?

What will be the most effective way of meeting goals?

Summary of Tasks to Consider in Engaging a Case Study

Familiarize Yourself with the Substance of the Case

Identify the Principal Issues

Note Objectives and Goals to Be Achieved

Identify Resources and Obstacles

Consider the Nature of Conflicts that Might Arise

Identify Dynamics of Behavior

Imagine Viable Alternative Ways of Proceeding

Evaluate Consequences of Proposed Decisions and Actions

Brainstorm Effective Strategies to Move Forward

Practice 5. Construct a Plan of Action

The case study is a tool to assist the group in grasping the complexity of the issue and possible steps toward its resolution. Processes used to engage the case study are a key factor in building a community of wisdom and mining the riches of the group. Constructing a plan of action, however, is a task too large for the whole group. The development and implementation of a plan of action requires particular leadership skills and careful design.

Leadership

A program of communal faculty development presupposes that the faculty exercises leadership within the institution. Competent in their fields, faculty members already possess a certain authority and status by virtue of their positions, yet this does not in itself guarantee an ability to get something done. Yet, as the Keystone Conferences taught us, when faculty members were discussing their passion—teaching—in an environment of mutual respect where everyone's time and talent were valued, their sense of leadership was clear and focused.

A Leadership Team

Institutions committed to communal faculty development might consider forming a leadership team of faculty that can include administrators, staff, and students as well. The task of the team is to take principal ownership for constructing and moving forward an action plan. Caution is in order, however, that the action not become or appear to be the "pet project" of a select few. That argues for ensuring that the formation of the team is as inclusive as possible. What might an institution bear in mind in suggesting people for the team?

Anyone familiar with group dynamics is aware of formal and informal authority. Although the academic dean may have the title, he or she may not be the authoritative voice among faculty members. Rather, the most senior faculty member or a person known for his or her particular expertise may be listened to more attentively. Team members must have the respect of their colleagues and be people proven trustworthy. Keystone participants suggested that "success is generated by enlisting a team of respected members of the faculty, that is, ones who have gained respect by speaking with wisdom and insight, evidencing a seriousness about the enterprise, listening to others, and embodying institutional virtues and getting things done; a group who will help the rest of the faculty to take ownership of the project by permitting it to evolve in grace, exhibiting enthusiasm, sharing a common body of information, and articulating change as movement toward a goal."[2] Those responsible for forming a team might keep the following points in mind.

Considerations for Putting Together a Leadership Team

Build a group that

1. Is grounded in the mission of the institution and knows the culture or ethos of the school.

2. Is conscious of the theological and vocational concerns of faculty members.

3. Has the potential for creative problem solving because it includes members with diverse thinking styles.

4. Enjoys respect among its peers.

5. Enjoys each other's company.

6. Will commit to working over a period of time, at times with intensity.

A Project Director

Naming a project director is helpful for the team and the project. One member of the team is chiefly responsible for calling meetings, ensuring that reports are completed, and generally keeping the ball rolling on a project of communal faculty development. A common complaint of faculty members is that issues raised over and over again seem to get lost after initial discussion. Appointing a team and particularly a project director is one way of keeping the issue on the front burner and entrusting someone specifically with the task of focusing the faculty's attention on it.

Elements of a Plan of Action

The team is in a position now to articulate a plan of action. Based on the tasks identified above that are part of a case analysis, the following elements shape a plan of action.

After the case study has been thoroughly analyzed and the team members have had a chance to listen to the input from the full faculty and other participants, the next step is to restate the issue contextualized within the institution.

Saint John's Seminary in Camarillo, California, for example, named their Keystone-related project, "Learning, Teaching, and Research for the Multicultural Church of the Southwest." Intent on addressing the multicultural dimension of their institution, the Camarillo team posed the following question as central to their project:

> How do we as the multicultural community of Saint John's Seminary accomplish the holistic formation of seminarians, which includes the scholarly task of the good theological school—learning, teaching, and research—in order to prepare more effective ministers for the multicultural church of the Southwest?

With this focus question, the leadership identified specific goals and strategies to achieve them.

NAME GOALS

Stated goals should be clear, realistic, and reasonable about what the faculty wants to achieve. Aiming too high can be a recipe for frustration. Identifying the resources available, the plan should articulate goals that reflect the concerns raised in conversations among faculty and other personnel and that respond to the challenge. Goals must also be measurable and capable of being assessed.

The Camarillo team identified four goals in response to their desire to address the multicultural reality of their institution:

Multicultural Reality as Resource. Whereas multiculturalism is often raised as a difficulty in the teaching and learning endeavor, this first goal emphasized multiculturalism as a resource, not a threat. Through a series of faculty colloquia the faculty explored multiculturalism by sharing personal experiences and reflecting on scholarly material on the subject.

Pedagogy and Adult Learning in Different Cultures. The faculty subsequently developed a library on multiculturalism and were required to define the multicultural aspects of their courses. Students were also encouraged to share their cultural experiences in the classroom setting. The goal challenged the faculty to explore issues of pedagogy and adult learning styles in different cultures.

Sensitivity to Cultural Diversity. Goal three was to implement teaching methods sensitive to cultural diversity. In one case, a faculty member allowed his class to be taped and offered it to the full faculty to view as a test case in cultural sensitivity within the classroom.

Evaluate Preparation for Multicultural Ministry. The final goal responded to the faculty's desire to know whether their graduates felt prepared for pastoral ministry in a multicultural context. They conducted a survey of alumni whose responses were used to evaluate the present program and to propose changes.

PLAN STRATEGIES

Taking into account the goals generated around an action plan as articulated, how might the goals be achieved? Planners should attend to skills available within the institution itself and also to those it needs to bring in from the outside. It is a truism that, even though faculty members work side by side, day in and day out, they rarely take time to share with each other what happens in their individual classrooms. There are master teachers in every faculty who are willing to share their experiences with their colleagues for the enrichment of the faculty as a whole and for the betterment of teaching and learning at their institution.

Keystone participants often invited experts in various fields to address the faculty and to serve as resource persons for their ongoing reflection on their issue in teaching and learning. Once again, the "stranger's voice" assisted them in understanding more fully the dilemma they faced and in proposing strategies to address it.

PRODUCE A TIMELINE FOR THE COMPLETION OF PHASES OF THE PROJECT

Deadlines can be a bane in the lives of busy people, yet they are essential. Setting a timeline provides a sense of accomplishment as the community makes progress in addressing its issue and noting the results with satisfaction. A timeline provides a schedule for work and a schedule for evaluation. Following it ensures the forward movement of the project, even if that may mean significant changes in goals and strategies.

It is not uncommon that an initial plan of action will be modified. New facts, new situations, and new obstacles all warrant reconsidering the plan and making necessary adjustments. If changes like these occur, institutions should be as careful to tap again into the wisdom community and to keep communication as open as it was at the start of the project. There is no easier way to lose the support of a group and insult the wisdom of the community than by making changes or redirecting a project without consultation.

Identify Persons Responsible for Tasks

Naming a team and a project leader is one way to ensure that a project does not get shelved. It is critical both in dealing with the overall project and each of the activities and strategies planned, that persons be named for specific tasks within a timeline. Tapping into the particular skills of the faculty, staff, and administration, the project leader or the team can solicit the assistance of a variety of people and thereby keep the project in the hands of the whole faculty and institution. There is always a risk that projects become the domain of a chosen few so staying alert to ways of engaging the whole wisdom community both as participants and as leaders can spell the difference between success and failure.

Plan a Process of Evaluation

Former New York City mayor Edward Koch became famous for his question: "How am I doing?" Evaluation is important as an affirmation and a corrective. No faculty would enter into a process of communal faculty development if members did not have a desire to become better at their craft as teachers. No parish community should pursue a project that will require a deep commitment of its members without a desire to keep track of its progress.

Evaluation or assessment determines the effectiveness of our efforts and fosters clarity of purpose and goals. Evaluation provides an opportunity to review the initial proposal in light of ongoing developments. Taking the time to evaluate throughout the project can serve as a corrective. Assumptions underlying the timeline can be checked and affirmed or challenged. Must the plan be altered? Have people fulfilled the responsibilities assigned them? Where is the project progressing well and where is it bogged down? Ongoing evaluations also provide the opportunity to name other issues that will require attention in the future. Sharing the results of any evaluation broadly keeps everyone abreast of the movement of the project and of their own role in carrying it forward.

Practice 6. Budget

A significant factor in any program of faculty development is the financial resources available for such an endeavor. Committing funds for communal faculty formation is a significant long-term investment, solidifying the faculty (or a parish staff) as a community of wisdom, and strengthening institutional effectiveness in light of its mission.

Words of Advice to Faculty and Administrators from Keystone Participants

Representatives from the twenty schools participating in the Keystone Conferences were asked what advice they would offer administrators and faculties considering a program of communal faculty development. The following points summarize their comments.

Advice to Administrators

1. Administrators must communicate and emphasize mission at all levels—individual, course, and program.

2. Action projects should arise from and be integrated with the culture of the institution and other things already going on in the life of the institution.

3. Be sensitive to the timing of the project. Regulate the pace and rhythm of the process for the faculty so that momentum is preserved and project goals and their completion remain in sight.

4. Keep the meaning of projects in front of the faculty, providing an overview of what the faculty is addressing and how the issues are related to each other.

5. Keep the project of faculty development "on the front burner" as an institutional priority and make time for it.

6. Engage consultants who can lend objectivity and provide an off-site place to gather from time to time.

7. Keep in mind faculty workload and be realistic in expectations; listen to the faculty and be willing to modify the project based on faculty input.

8. Name a project manager.

Advice for Faculty

1. Leadership in the project will be enhanced if there is a clear delineation of responsibility and power within a spirit of collegiality.

2. Faculty leadership ought to keep the project in the public eye; invest in the original vision of the project and communicate it while offering unique ways/insights to further develop it.

3. Anticipate revision of the project as it is implemented.

4. Allow the project to have priority in your work as part of your commitment to a common enterprise

5. Be collaborative. Individual faculty development is important, but ultimately not sufficient; involve the whole faculty and whole student body.

6. Invite faculty members to identify specific personal goals within the context of the broader program of communal faculty development, making explicit how the project will impact them and their work.

Conclusion

This chapter began by contrasting the effectiveness of "the power of one" with that of a community. Caught up in the details of a blueprint for faculty development, one might well lose sight of the central insight proven year after year at the Keystone Conferences: rarely do we sufficiently recognize and tap into the wisdom of those with whom we work. Faculty members were often pleasantly surprised to hear the creative teaching methods of a team colleague whom they somehow presumed was working with lecture notes forty years old and giving little thought to pedagogy.

Whether we are addressing dilemmas faced by faculties in theological education or parish communities running into obstacles in living as a community of faith, the ideas presented here can be of great assistance in assessing issues and moving toward their resolution. The unanticipated gift in the process is the development of a community of wisdom, of trust, and of strength that draws on the countless gifts of its members and moves them forward together for the good of the institution and the fulfillment of its mission.

NOTES

1. These points taken from Sharon A. McDade, *An Introduction to the Case Study Method: Preparation, Analysis and Participation* (Cambridge, Mass.: Harvard University, 1988).

2. Transcript, Keystone Conference 2000.

CHAPTER 6

Responding to Challenges in Theological Education as a Community of Wisdom: Processes for Faculty Development

---

Introduction

> When I imagine the community of truth gathered around some great thing—from DNA to *The Heart of Darkness* to the French Revolution—I wonder: Could teachers gather around the great thing called "teaching and learning" and explore its mysteries with the same respect we accord any subject worth knowing?[1]

This chapter offers specific processes that were employed either during the course of the Keystone Conferences and/or subsequently by participating schools to help to analyze case studies or to delve more deeply into issues related to teaching and learning. These processes can be adapted to different settings as tools to assist groups in examining a variety of issues and formulating responsive action plans. The chapter draws on specific strategies employed by Keystone faculty teams as they designed and implemented projects.

These processes and strategies, however, are not an elixir. Parker Palmer is helpful in this regard:

> There are no formulas for good teaching, and the advice of experts has but marginal utility. If we want to grow in our practice [as teachers] we have two primary places to go: to the inner ground from which good teaching comes and to the community of fellow teachers from whom we can learn more about ourselves and our craft.[2]

The processes collected here often ask group participants to reflect on their own experience and to share it with others. Counting on the experience, wisdom, and common goal of all those gathered, these tools for discussion, analysis, and action may be of great assistance to groups as they frame conversations about issues that are important to them.

Essential Conditions for Developing and Implementing Successful Processes

There are five preliminary factors to consider when developing and using processes for group work: (1) have a clear goal in mind; (2) be flexible with the process; (3) vary the process; (4) appoint someone to lead small groups; and (5) provide all materials participants will need.

Have a Clear Goal in Mind

Everyone has had the experience of being asked to work in a small group when the goal of the exercise was not clear. Even though it may be enjoyable, the conversation usually wanders aimlessly and endlessly. Participants leave the session frustrated because they were never sure what they were to discuss and accomplish. Having a clear goal is critical for designing and facilitating group process. It respects the participants' investment of time by being explicit about the purpose of the exercises.

Be Flexible with the Process

Those entrusted with facilitation of a group necessarily feel a great sense of responsibility and want to ensure that the process goes well. Consequently, they work hard designing processes that they believe will be most beneficial to the group. However, should a particular exercise not work despite diligent planning, facilitators must be flexible in adapting the process to the actual situation. Processes are instruments to achieve specific goals, not ends in themselves.

Vary the Process

Groups need variety in their work. In addition to the tasks to be accomplished in a particular process, one can vary process by alternating between large group and small group discussions. Depending on the goal of the process, organizers might want to arrange small groups to represent the interests of the constituents in a case study. Educational institutions, for instance, might view a case from the perspective of administrators, faculty, or students. A parish staff might work with a case taking the stance of various ethnic groups or diverse ministries within the parish community. Working in this way keeps the discussion fresh and energy high.

Appoint Someone to Lead Small Groups

When working in small groups, make sure that one person in each small group is aware of what the task is and how to lead the group through it in the time allotted. Someone else can be asked to serve as recorder to provide a follow-up report to the large group. If the small group will be meeting more than once, members might rotate the role of facilitator and recorder.

Provide All Material the Participants Will Need

Make sure that participants have all they need to fulfill their tasks. This can include newsprint, markers, and notepads—whatever will assist the work of the group.

Methods of Breaking Open Case Studies

There are various ways to enter a case study. The following processes have been field tested and refined at the Keystone Conferences.

Entering into a Dilemma with Imagination: Fishbowl

The *fishbowl exercise* is particularly helpful in familiarizing the group with the substance of a case by means of role playing. Several participants assume the roles of the characters in the case and surface the principal issues of concern while trying to capture the interpersonal dynamics of the characters.

> **Goal:** To allow group participants to involve themselves literally in the narrative of a case study as a way of entering into the various perspectives presented and moving toward a resolution of the dilemma.

Method:

The fishbowl exercise may be used in a variety of ways in order to make a case study come alive. It is called a fishbowl because the "actors" initially sit surrounded by other members of the group. They role play the dilemma in the personae of the characters as the larger group watches the action unfold. The "actors" adopt the concerns and attitudes of the principal players in the case study.

An interesting variation on the fishbowl process is to invite other participants from the group to come forward and take over the role of one of the "actors." One does this simply by tapping one of the actors on the shoulder who surrenders his or her seat and allows a new voice to be heard.

What does the fishbowl accomplish? It allows for an imaginative entry into a dilemma in a fairly safe atmosphere. It could be set up in such a way that participants are asked to assume the role of a character that holds an opposing view to their own. This exercise invites participants to appreciate the diverse perspectives at work in a dilemma. It does not immediately lead to a resolution, but it allows participants to enter into the dilemma in a way that might reveal solutions otherwise overlooked.

Uncovering Issues: Digging Deeper

This process tries to surface all the issues that might be at work in a particular case study. It underscores the importance of a well-written case that is thick in its description of the situation under consideration.

> **Goal:** To allow participants to work with a case study in order to get a sense of the multiple layers of issues that are at work and how they contribute to the dilemma.

Method:

This process uses questions to go deeper into a case study. Imagine a faculty discussing the issue of their workload. Within the large group are faculty, administrators, staff, and perhaps even students. This large group should be divided into smaller groups, mixing the various constituencies. The issue, while of utmost importance for the faculty, touches on the other constituents of the institution as well.

1. Spend the first fifteen minutes raising issues within the small groups. Assume that the issue is about workload. A guiding question for this brief exercise might be: "What is at work in the case that contributes to the problem?" The person most directly affected by the issue (in this case, a faculty member) might participate in the discussion but be present primarily as a listener and the one who will record what he or she heard for a report back to the large group.

2. For the next half-hour, the small groups address two questions:
   a. How do we individually deal with a heavy workload?
   b. How does the institution contribute to the problem or to the solution?

3. For fifteen minutes the recorders in each group are asked to report three things that they heard that ring true to them.

4. As the discussion comes to a close, the whole group responds to the question: "What else is at play?" At this point, participants can raise other issues and ask questions about the problem or its solution. They are asked to reflect on whether there is anything else going on that has been missed.

This process of digging deeper does not lead to specific solutions to a dilemma but rather helps the participants hear different voices on the issue. Those perspectives are essential for illuminating what steps toward a resolution of the problem may be available.

Processes Designed for Specific Areas

The following processes respond to particulars issue related to faculty development. Nonetheless, they have utility as well for religious educators who are trying to step back from the routines of ministry to reflect on specific goals and action plans. Or a group of preachers might substitute the word "preach" for "teach" as they adapt the process for reflecting on what they are actually doing when they preach.

Focus on Pedagogical Philosophy and Practice: Part I

Goal: To elicit from participants their own pedagogical understanding.

Method:

1. Prior to gathering, members of the faculty reflect individually on the following questions:

   a. How do I teach?
      - What is my "practice" of teaching?
      - What is the style or range of methods that I employ in my teaching, for example, lecture, dialogue, and small groups?
      - How do I arrange the classroom space?
      - What types of assignments do I give?

   b. Why do I teach this way?
      - Why is this my practice?
      - Does my method have a particular goal or goals?
      - What is my philosophy of education?
      - Why do I do what I do in class preparation, in the design of syllabi, in grading, in types of assignments?

   c. How has diversity changed the way I teach?
      - What are the kinds of diversity I attempt to deal with in the classroom?
      - How has diversity impacted my teaching, my understanding of education, and my teaching style(s)?
      - Which of these kinds of diversity have had the most and the least impact on me as a teacher?

2. At the faculty gathering, members divide into assigned small groups whose composition should be established by the organizing committee to get a mix of academic disciplines in each group. The purpose of the conversation is the conversation itself. It is an attempt to get faculty more consciously in touch with their current educational philosophy and pedagogical practices and to share them with their colleagues. Forty-five minutes to an hour can be set aside for this part of the process. There is no scheduled time to report the discussion to the large group.

3. Quiet time is set aside at the end of the discussion period for individuals to jot down their thoughts on newsprint provided by the team and organized under two headings: (1) What insights has this conversation provided for me? (2) What questions has this conversation raised for me? Each group posts their responses.

Focus on Pedagogical Philosophy and Practice: Part II

> **Goal:** To reflect on the type of student/minister one is trying to form in light of the institution's mission and to reflect on how one's own teaching and the teaching efforts of colleagues complement one another in this common task.

Method:

1. Prior to the gathering, ask faculty members to jot down some notes on the following questions:

   a. What kind of minister are we trying to form at our institution?
      - How would I describe the minister I am hoping to prepare by my teaching?
      - What vision of ministry ought s/he to have?
      - What principal skills does the minister need?
      - What level of integration can we expect of the student?

   b. How/what does my teaching contribute to the common good of the school?
      - How does my teaching contribute to preparation for ministry?
      - What assumptions about teaching and its outcomes do I bring to this task?
      - How do my pedagogical methods contribute to this preparation?

   c. How do my colleagues complement/complete my teaching?
      - How do I see that my colleagues contribute to preparation for ministry?
      - How do they complement what I do?
      - How do they challenge what I do?

2. At the faculty gathering, members meet in assigned small groups that reflect a mix of disciplines. For forty-five minutes to an hour the groups share their reflections on the preceding questions. There is no report back to the large group.

3. The process concludes with a quiet period at the end of the discussion with the opportunity for individuals to focus on two questions: (1) What do I see as the commonalities/diversity of the

visions presented? (2) What do I see as the commonalities/diversity of the pedagogies used to implement these visions? Responses from individuals are solicited in a plenary session.

Focus on Pedagogy

Often, teachers are unaware of the pedagogical practices of their colleagues. The following process encourages faculty members to share "success" stories in the classroom and to benefit from the wisdom and practices of each other.

> **Goal:** To identify significant moments in teaching and to analyze what contributed to their effectiveness in teaching and learning.

Method:

1. People prepare for the session using this question: What recent moment in class has created significant intellectual or emotional power for you as teacher?

2. Allot one hour for work in small groups to cover these two steps:
   a. Each person takes a turn identifying a moment of significance in her or his teaching
      - Note the common elements
      - Is the moment about something that happened for learners or for teachers?
      - Is the moment related to methods used or the subject matter?
   b. Try to get beneath the surface of the stories
      - What helped create the special moment of learning? What was happening?
      - Was it integrative learning—that is, did students begin to see connections?
      - Was it marked by analysis or synthesis?
      - Was it personal conversion?
      - What sort of feelings did it evoke?

3. Allot thirty to forty-five minutes in the large group to complete the following:

    a. Individually share what people heard or learned in their groups that was helpful to them concerning their own situation.

    b. How might that kind of learning be fostered? Can it be replicated?

4. Close the session by inviting participants to articulate strategies to address important issues raised: In light of the discussion, what specific steps can we take to facilitate teaching and learning?

Focus on Pedagogy/Diversity

Another process that might be used by faculties to tap into their teaching and learning skills relies on sharing successful moments especially regarding issues of diversity.

> **Goal:** To recall how one responded in the classroom to the challenge of diversity—whether due to academic ability, cultural difference, or educational background—in order to generate advice for other teachers.

Method:

1. Spend fifteen minutes surfacing issues by asking the following question:
   - What issues present themselves in the classroom because of diversity due to academic ability, theological stance, cultural difference, educational background, or personality differences?

2. Spend forty-five minutes in small groups focused on the following task:
   - Relate an incident about how you changed your teaching in response to student differences.
   - What did you learn?

3. For one half hour in large group, share responses using the following question as a starting point:
   - Based on the discussion in small groups, what advice would you offer other teachers facing similar issues?

Focus on Tapping the Diversity of the Student Body as a Resource

Several institutions participating in the Keystone Conferences pointed to the diversity of their student body as a challenge in theological education. The same institutions, however, were intent on identifying this diversity as a treasure, not a burden. The following process enables teachers to listen to their students and to gain insights into the diversity of needs before them. The focus of this exercise is on the educational experiences of students from different cultures. A parish staff responding to multiple cultures around liturgical needs could adapt this process for its deliberations.

> **Goal:** To understand the multicultural reality as a resource and to explore issues, like pedagogy and adult learning styles, from within the perspective of different cultures.

Method:

1. Faculty members meet with students who represent the diverse cultures in the school. In one instance, the faculty met with twelve students representing six different cultures (Hispanic, Vietnamese, Korean, African, Filipino, Euro-American). The students come prepared to respond to these questions:

   a. What effective learning skills have you developed?

   b. Based on your academic history as a learner, what teaching style have you found most helpful to you?

   c. Do you pursue learning on your own? What kinds of learning resources (library, videos, books, research materials, etc.) do you need for this?

   d. From the perspective of your culture, describe what it means to be a learner. Is there anything else that would be helpful for teachers to know about your culture and how it impacts your life as a student here?

   e. What methods of accountability have been most helpful in your learning?

2. Student panelists are given approximately ten to fifteen minutes each to respond to the questions.

3. Faculty break into small groups for about one hour. Student representatives will be present to clarify and share in the conversation. Questions for faculty groups:
   - What insights did the student presentations offer?
   - What are the challenges we face in assuring effective pedagogy?
   - What might we do to deepen our awareness?

4. The large group gathers for one half hour to explore what people learned from the workshop, what questions remain, and what the next steps will be.

Focus on Conversion

Faculty members frequently comment on a gap between themselves and their students. Sometimes this is due to diversity of culture, language, educational background, theological stance, spirituality, or a host of other factors. This experience of distance can lead to tension and wondering on the part of the teacher, "How can I get them to change?" It is a common question in most communities where divisions rise up because of a wide range of differences.

In the Keystone experiences, some faculty expressed particular frustration in dealing with closed or rigid students. What emerged from subsequent discussion was a realization that for the sake of genuine learning there must be a change in both teacher and student. Although conversion cannot be mandated, the following process might assist faculties to identify elements of change or conversion and to move toward strategies that foster mutual growth.

> **Goal:** To understand the dynamics/elements of conversion in one's own life in order to facilitate the process of conversion for oneself and others.

Method:

1. People gather in small groups with these instructions: Please relate an incident or story about how you changed your mind about another person, a particular student, or a situation in your own life. Each person has about five minutes to respond.

2. After the members of the small group have listened to one another's stories of conversion, reflect on the following question: As you listened to the stories, what dynamics were operative in this "conversion process"? Allot about fifteen minutes for this part of the process.

3. Return to the large group to share insights regarding dynamics of conversion raised in the smaller groups.

4. Conclude the session by asking what strategies seem implicit in the conversations for moving oneself and others toward change.

Focus on Curriculum Revision

Institutions that face curriculum change know that they are facing a daunting task. They may not know how to begin. The Saint Paul Seminary School of Divinity faculty surfaced some helpful questions as they entered into a process of curriculum revision. Their questions might serve as a starting point for similar discussions at other schools.

> **Goal:** To analyze the constitutive values and assumptions of a curriculum.

Method:

Pose these questions for institution-wide discussion:
- Should the curriculum be content based or learner based? Why?
- Should emphasis be placed on disciplinary integrity or pastoral application? Why?
- Is the goal to develop scholars or pastoral leaders or both?
- Is a professional curriculum less academic than a traditional graduate curriculum or simply academically different? In what ways?
- Does the integrating factor of the curriculum lie in one of the traditional theological disciplines (for example, liturgy) or in an area of pastoral skill (for examples, homiletics)? Is one preferable to the other? Why?
- Should the school provide a close-ended system of learning in which we attempt to teach everything that is needed or an

open-ended system that equips students to be self-directed life-long learners? What are the advantages/disadvantages of each?

- How can personal and spiritual formation proceed side-by-side with academic training while using the same faculty?
- Do we program for short-range needs of constituents or for a long-range, research-based vision of church and parish life or for both?

Focus on Curriculum Assessment and Revision

In addition to an internal review of their operative assumptions about the curriculum, the Saint Paul Seminary School of Divinity faculty consulted broadly with their constituents prior to revising their curriculum. Meetings were held with sponsoring bishops and their staffs, with pastors of past and future graduates, with lay leaders of parishes, and with alumni. The following questions can offer ideas for how best to structure meetings of this nature.

Goal: To listen to constituents' views about the curriculum and its relationship to pastoral needs.

Method:

Arrange meetings with the various constituents served by the institution in order to assess the effectiveness of the curriculum in light of the graduates' preparedness for ministry. Questions that might be asked in meetings with constituents named above are as follows:

1. Questions to be asked at diocesan-level meetings:
   - What are the most significant challenges a new priest will face in this diocese?
   - What role can the seminary play in helping prepare students to meet those challenges?
   - What are your priorities in terms of seminary formation?
   - What qualities/assets/talents seem to stand out in our recent graduates?
   - As we continue to work with and form lay ministers, are there particular concerns you would have about the structure and content of the program we offer?

2. Questions to be asked in meetings with pastors:
   - What are the essential qualities, skills, and abilities a seminarian will need to work effectively as a priest of this diocese? Will these change in any way during the next ten years? How might they change?
   - How have your expectations of the newly ordained from any seminary been met, surpassed, or gone unfulfilled?
   - What issues of parish life should we be most aware of as we plan or improve our programs?
   - How would you compare those priests you know who were ordained in the past five years with priests ordained fifteen to twenty years ago?
   - On the basis of your experience, what expectations would you have of programs providing graduate-level preparation for lay ministry?

3. Questions to be asked in meetings with lay leaders:
   - What are three or four indispensable expectations you have of a parish priest?
   - What leadership qualities will a priest need to serve this diocese in the next ten years?
   - What expectations do you have of lay people who serve the church as professional lay ministers?
   - What motivates you to be active in your parish?
   - What do you expect from a "good homily"?

4. Questions to be asked at meetings with graduates:
   - For which aspects of parish ministry were you best prepared?
   - For which aspects of parish ministry were you least or under prepared?
   - What particular challenges have you experienced as you have worked with lay ministry colleagues (or with clergy)?

Focus on Curriculum Assessment for Ministerial Responsibility

The following process is helpful for faculties who periodically review their curriculum in light of the mission of the institution and their stated goals. The framework for this process (see Figure 1) includes in the vertical column the areas of expertise in ministry that an institution seeks to develop. In the horizontal column are the typical academic disciplines/departments. A parish staff could adapt this process to include various pastoral tasks in the vertical column and list the ministries of the parish community on the horizontal level.

> **Goal:** To articulate the goals for ministry that an institution hopes to foster and to identify what each field of study can contribute to each area of ministerial responsibility.

Method:

Using Figure 1 as the framework (and adapting it as needed to the particular situation of the institution), faculty members first work individually and then as departments to link their course offerings with the ministerial skills identified in the vertical column.[3]

1. Faculty members individually review their own course offerings in light of the goals for ministry (twenty minutes).

2. Departments or program areas meet together to compare how each member sees his or her courses contributing to the formation of the minister (forty-five minutes).

3. In a plenary session, the whole faculty hears the reports from the individual departments or program areas (twenty minutes).

4. Having heard the reports, the faculty addresses the following questions (thirty minutes):
   a. In what ways are we fulfilling our task in formation for ministry?
   b. Where are there gaps in the present curriculum?
   c. Who might be responsible for addressing these gaps and in what way?

Focus on Curriculum Assessment by Students

Institutions spend months, even years, working on curriculum revision hoping to produce a curriculum that facilitates their mission and produces graduates well versed in theology and prepared for ministry. Once a new curriculum is in place, feelings of relief can move administration and faculty to forget about assessment. How is the curriculum working? Is it fulfilling our expectations? The following exercise can be

Figure 1

Creating a Framework for Assessing Curriculum

Field of Study / Area of Ministerial Responsibility	Historical Studies *Historical Theology Spiritual Theology*	Scriptural Studies *Sacred Scripture*	Theological Studies *Systematic Theology Moral Theology*	Pastoral Studies *Min. of Word/ Sacrament Ministry to Church/Society*
Preaching				
Worship				
Teaching				
Pastoral Care				
Administration/ Congregational Leadership				
Public Leadership and Ecumenical Relations				
Multicultural/ Immigration/ Language Issues				

used with small groups of students as a way to elicit their input on the adequacy of a revised curriculum.

> **Goal:** To facilitate student assessment of the adequacy of curriculum goals.

Method:

Gather students for an informal lunch, small group meeting, or even as a panel at a faculty meeting. Participating students should have the questions in advance so that they have time to prepare responses. Questions can be adapted in light of an institution's curriculum.

1. What are your general impressions of the ways in which the curriculum fits together?

2. What would be the most significant insight into theology that you have gained this year?

3. As a result of your studies thus far, what are the distinctive marks of the Catholic intellectual tradition?

4. How have your studies affected you personally this year especially regarding your sense of and orientation to ministry?

Focus on Integration

The theme of integration typically focuses on forming a person humanly, spiritually, pastorally, and intellectually. A faculty might attend, therefore, to how these four dimensions of formation are addressed in the academic and formation curricula of the school. Faculty might also tackle the issue of integration by considering the type of graduate it hopes to produce through the formation process.

> **Goal:** To identify the type of graduate an institution hopes to form and educate and to reflect on how faculty as individuals and as a group achieve this outcome.

Method:

1. In several small groups or one large group, ask participants to identify their "ideal graduate," taking into account three areas: knowledge, attitudes, and skills.

2. Give participants time to reflect by themselves on how they contribute to the shaping of this graduate; then ask them to reflect on what the institution does.

3. Note areas that need attention in light of the description of the graduate and the actual reality of the institutional and faculty practices.

Guiding Questions for a Comprehensive Examination of the Challenges in Theological Education

The questions that follow guided evaluative discussions at the Keystone Conferences. In response to these questions, participants offered principles and practices to their colleagues that are reflected in the opening chapters in this book: student diversity, integration, and assessment. Participants considered these three issues from five perspectives: classroom pedagogy, learning environment, curriculum, ministry, and faculty development (see Figures, 2, 3, and 4).

- While *pedagogy* focuses on the individual classroom, hopefully a strong argument has been made for the benefit of tapping into the wisdom community of colleagues. Crossing over the threshold of the classroom and sharing pedagogical efforts for the good of the students build a synergy of effort that significantly advances the mission of the school.

- Over the years, we have become acutely aware of the importance of the *learning environment*. How is the theme of diversity, which is both a challenge and a blessing, manifest in such things as the artwork used in campus buildings, music at daily liturgies, or in the staffing practices of institutions?

- Educational institutions recognize the critical necessity of maintaining a solid *curriculum* to meet the needs of students and broader constituents. This calls for a flexibility borne of attentiveness and ongoing institutional self-critique.

- Every school of theological education offers degrees in *ministry*. This aspect of the mission of the institution must be evident in the quality and method of teaching and learning in an integral way.

- The challenges posed by student diversity, integration, and assessment weigh heavily on faculty. It would be unthinkable to build strategies of action without including a strong commitment to *faculty development*. The image of creating a community of wisdom for faculty development emphasizes the power found in the expertise and passion of faculty working as a group.

Goal: To examine challenges in theological education through a multifaceted lens so as to grasp the complexity of the challenge and the breadth of the response needed.

Method:

Work in small groups on the questions posed in handouts based on Figures 2, 3, and 4.

Figure 2

The Challenge of Diversity

	DIVERSITY
Classroom Pedagogy	What are the implications of diversity for class-room pedagogy? How has your awareness of diversity changed your teaching? How has your understanding of how students learn changed your teaching?
Learning Environment	What are the implications of diversity for the learning environment? What has changed in your learning environment because of your awareness of diversity and who was responsible for bringing these changes? What else could/should change?
Curriculum	What are the implications of diversity for the curriculum? What curricular changes in structures and/or content have you made to address diversity and why have you made them? What helpful processes led to the changes?
Ministry	What issues related to ministry arise regarding diversity and how have you addressed them? How are cultural, linguistic, and educational backgrounds addressed in light of future ministry? What are the implications of diversity in ministerial settings?
Faculty Development	What are the implications of diversity for faculty development? What issues arose for faculty development because of the diverse student body and what initiatives were taken, collectively and individually, to address them? How does any diversity on the faculty itself affect faculty development?

Figure 3

The Challenge of Integration

	INTEGRATION
Classroom Pedagogy	What are the implications of integration for classroom pedagogy? How do your teaching methods promote integration? What shape do any of your integrating activities take, especially your final integrating activity?
Learning Environment	What are the implications of integration for the learning environment? How is/could integration (be) valued and modeled by the institution?
Curriculum	What are the implications of integration for the curriculum? What curricular changes in structures and content have you made to support integration?
Ministry	What are the implications of integration for formation for ministry? What is integration in this regard, why do we value it, what does it look like? How does your institution help students integrate aspects of their formation?
Faculty Development	What are the implications of integration for faculty development? How have faculty been helped to foster integration in the students and in the program? How do faculty themselves integrate the various dimensions of formation?

Figure 4

The Challenge of Assessment

	ASSESSMENT
Classroom Pedagogy	What are the implications of assessment for classroom pedagogy? What assessment tools have you used to foster learning?
Learning Environment	What are the implications of assessment for the learning environment? How do you assess an effective learning environment? How has the learning environment of your school changed as a result of assessment?
Curriculum	What are the implications of assessment for the curriculum? How have you assessed the efficacy of your curriculum?
Ministry	What are the implications of assessment for formation for ministry? How do you judge whether students are equipped for the church's ministries? What related issues arise?
Faculty Development	What are the implications of assessment for faculty development? How has your faculty learned to improve assessment methods? What tools does the institution use to assess faculty performance?

Conclusion

This chapter serves as a practical guide for group work with faculties, parish staffs, and others intent on working together as a community. The practicality of these exercises should not obscure their deeper twofold result: greater insight into issues under examination and deepened respect for and appreciation of the other members of the group. Simple, well-designed processes allow for sharing of experiences that go beyond merely voicing opinions, precisely because they evoke the passion that shapes participants' lives.

Parker Palmer remarks that "The resources we need in order to grow as teachers are abundant within the community of colleagues."[4] The resources that faculties, parish staff, administrators, and others need to grow as a community of wisdom are within their community of colleagues. The tools presented here open that wisdom up to public view.

NOTES

1. Parker Palmer, *The Courage to Teach: Exploring the Inner Landscape of a Teacher's Life* (San Francisco: Jossey-Bass Publishers, 1998) 141.

2. Ibid.

3. This graph was developed by Sr. Katarina Schuth, O.S.F.

4. Parker Palmer, ibid., 144.

CHAPTER 7

What Technology Can Teach about Theological Pedagogy

Thomas Esselman, C.M.

Perhaps nothing has so dramatically affected issues of pedagogy as the emergence of educational technology. The use of the computer as a tool for teaching and learning has evoked strong feelings among faculties who often experience the prospect of implementing instructional technology as a source of "fear and trembling." This chapter examines whether instructional technologies can be responsibly and creatively used in the work of theological teaching and learning for ministry. It also explores some of the common theological and pedagogical concerns raised by faculty members using technology in teaching and learning, the issues of teaching practice, and the work of one theological school that has implemented Web technologies in its on-campus and distance education programs. The chapter concludes with reflections on how technology might aid theological teaching and learning in meeting the challenges of diversity, integration, and assessment.

Emerging Technologies for Theological Teaching and Learning

Between 1997 and 1999, the Lilly Endowment Inc., awarded grants totaling twenty-five million dollars to seventy-two theological schools for the purpose of developing the use of instructional technologies.[1] This grant initiative was a signal event in the recent history of theological education. It equipped a significant number of Catholic, Protestant, and Orthodox schools with the resources to begin or continue the process of integrating the use of technology into their respective teaching missions.[2]

Some schools, for example, have wired their campus buildings for e-mail and Internet access. Others have upgraded their preaching classrooms or are working to put parts or all of their library holdings online. Many schools have purchased computers, printers, and scanners for faculty and staff and developed new technology labs, staffed by full or part-time technology coordinators. Some schools have outfitted their classrooms for in-class access to the Internet and regular use of multimedia presentation programs such as PowerPoint. Augmenting all of these institutional investments there is, of course, the ever-improving technology of the personal computer. Anyone with a reliable computer, Internet access, and a browser has writing and research tools that were unavailable to scholars just a few years ago.

Theologically Appropriate and Pedagogically Effective

The "fear and trembling" that colleagues in theological education often associate with technology is based on something more than the technical challenges of learning how to use computers, databases, and the Internet. Underlying the concerns of theologians are questions about the theological appropriateness and the pedagogical effectiveness of technology. These questions are of fundamental importance, for they reflect deeper convictions of theologians concerning the nature of theology, the embodied character of learning, and the standards of intellectual, ministerial, and spiritual development expected of those preparing for ministry. To discuss technology's place in theological education, one needs to explore some of the issues at stake.

Theological Appropriateness

A first issue concerns the location of theological teaching and learning within the wider ecclesial tradition of life and practice. Theological formation for ministry is an integrative process of personal transformation anchored in the deep mysteries of faith as they are known and lived out in the tradition of the church. Candidates for ministry enter into rigorous and critical theological inquiry and into development of the skills needed to be effective pastoral agents. At the same time, they are challenged to grow in holiness and assume the habits of a spirituality that support ministerial service in the church. This integrative process of transformation finds its center of gravity in the revelation of the triune God as the heart of the universe and the source of all true praise.

Word, sacrament, ritual, and the concrete exercise of love in community mediate God's revelation. It is in the context of this mystery of God revealed that the church is formed, ministers discover their calling, and theology is called to critical reflection in the world.

Given the deeply personal and embracing nature of revelation and the inadequacy of any human attempt to ever adequately express this mystery, is it appropriate to use instructional technology in theological teaching? Are digital media able to capture the richness of life that is "practiced" in the Christian tradition? Can an online discussion among learners in virtual space, for example, represent the mysteries of faith in a meaningful and theologically appropriate manner?

A second issue regarding the theological appropriateness of technology concerns the pedagogical challenge of cultivating in ministry students a spirit of pastoral wisdom. The goal of theological education is more than simply an increase in knowledge, skills, or holiness. Theological education aims at developing in students a deeper wisdom by which they are configured to a life of oblative service and prophetic vision in the church and in the world. Peter Hodgson defines such wisdom *(paideia)* as a blending of critical thinking, heightened imagination, and liberating practice.[3] Walter Burghardt notes that the kind of wise theologian the world desperately needs today is the man or woman who not only knows a theology of God but more importantly knows the God of theology.[4] Lois Malcolm reminds us that wisdom ultimately arises out of a fearless and authentic encounter with the complex powers at work in our world today. She writes:

> Seminaries need to be attentive to the fact that they are educating leaders for a very different world than the one they prepared students for in the past. The model of "apostolate" may be a more fruitful way of thinking about the design of the seminary than that of the "academy." At issue in this new context may not be the task of defending Christianity's cognitive claims as much as learning how to use spiritual powers appropriately. But that entails discerning God's justice and mercy in the full complexity of life, and to do that we cannot escape the difficult task of integrating the multiple dimensions of our lives.[5]

Theological education today emphasizes the importance of developing the habit of theological reflection as a means of cultivating this wisdom. Is the use of instructional technology compatible with this goal?

A third issue regarding the theological appropriateness of technology is rooted in a sacramental consciousness that appreciates the embodied nature of Christian life and its implications for teaching and learning. The basic paradigm of learning in the Christian tradition is that of a highly personal and immediate relationship between master and pupil. Jesus called disciples who followed him. Countless generations of Christians have organized themselves around this example. Undoubtedly, for many faculty and students in our theological schools, real learning takes place when students have the opportunity to mentor under a distinguished teacher. The reliability of this mentor-student model exists in tension with models of adult pedagogy that stress learning as a self-directed, cooperative venture. What does this suggest, for example, about the relationship between "real" (face-to-face) as opposed to virtual (computer-mediated) forms of presence in teaching and learning? If the teaching and learning experience presupposes a level of embodiment or sacramentality, is it theologically appropriate for faculty to design courses that depend, in part or in whole, on the virtual presence of learners to each other?

These are the kind of issues raised when faculty colleagues discuss the appropriateness of using technology in teaching from a theological perspective.[6] They form the broader context out of which theologians assess the use of technology in teaching and learning today.

Pedagogical Effectiveness

While the theological appropriateness of using technology in the classroom concerns seminary educators, they are equally concerned about its pedagogical effectiveness. Elizabeth Patterson has articulated what might be considered a first principle of good practice here: it is pedagogy that should direct the selection and use of technology in the classroom, not vice versa.[7] While the literature on the pedagogical implications of using technology in the theological classroom is only beginning to emerge, the issues involved are increasingly the topic of conversation among colleagues in the field.[8]

The central pedagogical concern is whether and how the use of technology contributes to deeper student learning and a more robust learning environment. It is this commitment to learning that persuades most theological faculties to take a cautious approach in adopting new technologies. There are significant issues to consider. Implementing new technologies in the curriculum is a labor-intensive activity. It challenges "tried and true" methods of teaching and learning with which some faculty and students have grown comfortable. Because of the need to consider in advance how the use of new technologies contribute to enhanced student learning, faculties need to design ongoing assessment strategies that measure the pedagogical effectiveness of technology in their courses and programs.

Another pedagogical concern in the use of technology is the issue of changing roles and relationships within the teaching and learning process. As instructors and students move from face-to-face to virtual learning environments, they inevitably experience how the medium reshapes roles and relationships within learning. A faculty member who is used to being at the "center of attention" in the classroom setting will find herself forced to rethink her role as she considers how to encourage interactivity among groups of students working together online. For pedagogues, a shift in roles and relationships can be exciting but also threatening. Faculties today need to carefully assess the impact that technology has on all the learners, instructors, as well as students.[9]

Another set of pedagogical concerns revolves around the selection, use, and maintenance of the technology itself. Amidst the abundant options available, faculties need to carefully choose the specific technologies that will support teaching and learning in their respective disciplines. The decision to invest in new technologies calls for a plan for ongoing student and faculty training and technical support. As Pallof and Pratt note, faculty and students need training that includes not only the "how to" of using various technologies, but, more importantly, an understanding of "what it takes to teach and learn online successfully."[10] The decision to invest in new technologies calls for the development of an institutional infrastructure that will support faculty and students in their use of the technology.[11] Any viable technology program requires a clear institutional plan to provide for its ongoing financial costs.

A final set of pedagogical concerns often cited relate to technology's impact on faculty load, morale, and the specific culture of the seminary community. Despite the bright promises of technology for improved teaching and learning, faculty members sometimes worry that the labor, time, and attention needed to implement it will cause other areas of professional service to suffer, such as research, publishing, and student assistance. Schools that have traditionally fostered theological study within the context of a strong, person-centered community life will undoubtedly need to reflect on the impact that technology has on that culture. In the end, the commitment to use technology in the curriculum has to be consistent with the faculty's self-identity as a community of theologians.

These particular pedagogical concerns highlight some of the complex issues that any theological faculty committed to using technology in the curriculum must address. Attentiveness to issues of theological appropriateness and pedagogical effectiveness are critical in the development of a successful technology program for teaching and learning. As Raymond Williams has written:

> A theological school must first tend to the pedagogical and theological challenges and potentials. Once it is certain of its mission and confident of the commitments and abilities of its faculty and students, it can shape technology to its purposes, rather than being distracted or even derailed by the technology.[12]

A Case Example:
The Pedagogy of the Online Wisdom Community

In recent years the faculty of Aquinas Institute of Theology, a Dominican-sponsored school of theology and ministry in St. Louis, Missouri, have been implementing creative uses of instructional technology in their degree programs. When a team of Aquinas faculty participated in the Keystone Conference in 1997, the school had just begun offering a distance education Master of Arts in Pastoral Ministry (MAPM) degree for dioceses in western states that lack traditional resources for theological training.[13] In the original design of the MAPM degree, faculty members traveled to extension sites in Oklahoma City and Colorado Springs for intensive weekend sessions with students. Before 1999, the degree was decidedly "low-tech," featuring neither video-conferencing nor Web-based teaching resources.

As a result of its participation in the Keystone Conferences, however, Aquinas began to explore the use of digital technologies in the design and delivery of this distance education degree. The faculty agreed to collaborate in a study of their distance education pedagogy in order to develop new ways of incorporating technology into the design of the MAPM degree. The project began during the spring of 1998 with a series of focused faculty discussions on what constitutes excellence in theological teaching and learning. Out of these conversations, the faculty were able to articulate a set of consensus principles on good theological pedagogy that would guide their decisions about the implementation of technology in their degree programs.

The Aquinas faculty concluded that good theological pedagogy consists of the following:

- a commitment to rapport: the development of respectful, constructive, and creative relationships among learners in real time;

- a commitment to experiential learning: pedagogy that relates theory to praxis in a way that helps students not only draw from the tradition but also experientially work out for themselves a sense of the activity of ministry;

- a commitment to self-directed learning: pedagogy that equips students with the essential resources to do theology, encourages them to take initiative in the production of knowledge, and challenges them to remain current in their chosen fields throughout their lives;

- a commitment to integration: learning that helps students appropriate the ecclesial and ministerial significance of the issues they study;

- a commitment to learning as a communal process: pedagogy that cultivates in learners an appreciation of the wider tradition from which they draw and the importance of their own contributions to that heritage today; and

- a commitment to the creation of "wisdom communities:" cultivation of wisdom that comes from participation in a learning community open to personal transformation.[14]

The faculty then redesigned the distance-learning program in light of these principles.

In the new design (right-hand side, Figure 1), faculty members continue to travel to the extension site and work in real time with the cohort of students. These face-to-face sessions remain central to the pedagogical design of the degree. However, in order to support and enhance rapport, a Web-based component of instruction has been introduced that allows instructor and students to continue their work online in the weeks when they are apart. As faculty members gained greater expertise with this model over time, they discovered new possibilities for teaching and learning. Web-based teaching allows for the

Figure 1

Using Web-based teaching in the redesign
of the distance education MAPM degree

MAPM degree design—without Web-based teaching (1995–1999)	Current MAPM degree design—with weekly Web-based teaching (1999–)
July 28—Students receive course syllabus; study in preparation for first intensive session	July 28–August 3 Online Week I
	August 4–10 Online Week II
	August 11–16 Online Week III
August 17—First Intensive Meeting in the Diocese	
Study in preparation for the intensive weekend	August 18-24 Online Week IV
	August 25–31 Online Week V
	September 1–6 Online Week VI
September 6, 7, 8—Intensive Weekend in the Diocese	
Study in preparation for the third intensive session; work on final course project (research paper or preparation for exam)	September 8–14 Online Week VII
	September 15–21 Online Week VIII
	September 22–27 Online Week IX
September 29—Third Intensive Session in the Diocese	

creation of virtual community. More importantly, the Web can be effectively used to structure and support the online learning cohort into a wisdom community for critical theological reflection. If the pedagogical principle of rapport suggests the limitations of technology in teaching and learning, the wisdom community ideal suggests new pedagogical possibilities.

The notion of the wisdom community in theological education has been developed by Mary Margaret Pazdan, O.P.[15] Drawing on her exegesis of wisdom in the Johannine and Pauline texts, she describes a model of collaborative and transformative learning that can be found in any number of settings in the life of the church. Wisdom communities "exist whenever and wherever persons gather intentionally to share life and commitment to Christian values in the presence of the Spirit."[16] For theological education, the wisdom community serves as a model for understanding the nature of teaching and learning that grows out of a process of critical reflection engaging instructors and students alike. Pazdan writes:

> The heart of theological education . . . is adult formation for ministry that includes rigorous intellectual efforts as well as deepening and expanding the faith of individuals who will be entrusted with the mission of the Church. Wisdom learning requires mutual attention to the tradition and formation of all who participate in collaborative, mutual learning. My experience of teaching biblical studies . . . for many years convinces me that the presence and nurturing of wisdom communities are essential for ecclesial growth and integrity.[17]

The challenge of theological teaching and learning, in face-to-face and in virtual settings, lies in the formation of vibrant wisdom communities.

It is out of this wisdom community model that the Aquinas faculty has developed its approach to Web-based teaching, focusing on ways to use the Internet so as to create and support online wisdom communities.[18] These online wisdom communities are pedagogically important in cohort degree programs where students at a distance work online in asynchronous learning units before and after intensive, face-to-face teaching sessions with the faculty person. They are also useful in the design of residential courses. Such online wisdom communities are always founded upon the cooperative learning of students and instructor who gather to work in real time.

The following examples demonstrate the development of an online wisdom community in different areas of the curriculum. Each example describes the goals of the course and pedagogical methods for helping an online wisdom community engage in theological reflection. The summary highlights lessons learned in light of concerns for theological appropriateness and pedagogical effectiveness when using technology.

Exploring Themes in Fundamental Theology with the Online Wisdom Community

Aquinas Institute's Master of Arts in Health Care Mission (MAHCM) degree is designed to offer practitioners in Catholic healthcare the foundational theological, ministerial, and spiritual training needed to serve as mission leaders in this ministry of the church. Students in the MAHCM degree live in various parts of the country and work full time in a variety of health care ministries. In order to make such a degree program possible, each MAHCM course is structured around a mid-course, on-campus intensive of four days; in the weeks before and after the intensive the students work online, using a course website designed by the Aquinas instructor.

The Introduction to Theology and Theological Method course provides "an introduction to the discipline of theology through an examination of fundamental issues such as faith, revelation, Scripture, tradition, doctrine and dogma, and theological method" (course syllabus). One of the goals of the course is the student's ability to "apply the foundations of theological thinking to current challenges in Catholic health care ministry" (course syllabus). While I have taught the Introduction to Theology course any number of times in the past, I was aware that in this instance most of the students had little formal background in theology. At the same time, they had impressive experience in various areas of Catholic healthcare ministry. Tapping into their experience could encourage a critical and lively conversation between the work of healthcare and fundamental issues of theology.

Two goals guided my layout of the website. First, the website had to be a user-friendly place for accessing a number of course resources. Second, the website structure needed to engage the students in an organized process of theological reflection, using focused discussion questions and the threaded discussion format as a key tool.[19]

One of the pedagogical challenges of designing for accessibility is the need to think through beforehand a range of issues such as the identity of the learners, the intended goals of the course, teaching strategies that will support these goals, the impact of course requirements on students, the availability of technical support, and how one will evaluate student work.

The more important pedagogical goal was that of encouraging interactivity around critical theological reflection. A series of different weekly topics and related readings, accompanied by an online discussion exercise, enabled students to speak with one another. Students were also organized into small online groups of four or five and assigned a weekly focus question. They met asynchronously on a threaded discussion board.

The weekly online discussion questions intentionally promoted the kind of critical theological reflection needed in the study of fundamental theology. At the same time, the discussions encouraged interactivity among the learners in accord with the model of a wisdom community.[20]

Thus, each weekly question began with an appeal to the student's experience, inviting him or her to name how a theological theme is enfleshed in the real-life situations and crises of today. In the context of these questions, participants engaged in a critical reading of the texts that make up the ecclesial and theological traditions so that they could reflect on and appropriate for themselves what others in the past have said. Very often, this kind of critical reading can be disturbing or unsettling, challenging the student to what Pazdan refers to as the "perspective of the second naiveté."[21]

It is at this point that students often struggle with the meaning of theological language and the hermeneutical issues of how to understand a particular text. They also encounter the challenge of rethinking their original understandings of a theme or text, a fact that very often becomes evident in the course of the group's online discussion. A final step in the design of the online questions moved the reflection one step forward: What new questions arise from one's critical reading of the tradition—and what new insights for Christian praxis emerge? In the case of this cohort, Catholic health care specialists reflected on the implications of their theological reflection for the current work of their ministry.

Richard Ascough notes, "At the core of the online learning experience is the experience for students to regularly participate in ongoing threaded discussions. More than any other aspect of the online environment, the asynchronous threaded discussions are a means to insure student-to-student interaction."[22] A well-designed use of threaded discussion boards can be a place of constructive and rich theological reflection where students contribute to the life of an emerging wisdom community. It is important to note that this Web-enhanced teaching format can easily be integrated into the design of a residential course to enhance the weekly face-to-face interactions of students.

Mentoring Pastoral Interns as an Online Wisdom Community

Ironically, students who spend a pastoral year or internship as part of master of divinity programs often find themselves with fewer resources for doing theological reflection than when they are on campus. Seminary faculty are all too familiar with the intern who returns from a placement in a parish or hospital and reports that, while the work was challenging and engaging, her supervisor was often unavailable or unable to engage in critical theological reflection. If field education directors are to help students cultivate the habit of theological reflection within active ministry, they will need to find ways to more directly engage interns while they are away from campus during full-time placements.

A project underway at Aquinas Institute adapts use of the Internet for gathering pastoral interns for on-going theological reflection as an online wisdom community. For both seminarians and lay students at Aquinas, the internship develops ministry skills and deepens one's authority and identity as a minister. It also seeks to help the student "learn and practice theological reflection on ministry experiences, both in a supervisory relationship and in a group setting" (course syllabus).

We use Web-based communication as one of the ways to bring the interns together as a wisdom community. The Web offers a medium that enables interns located in different cities and parts of the country to engage periodically in ongoing theological reflection. The website provides a forum where students can raise theological reflection issues and receive constructive feedback. Alternating turns, a student leader will post a critical incident drawn from his or her ministry experience on the website. The other members of the group are expected to post a substantive reflection on one aspect of the presented incident. These substantive responses might include:

- An identification of the theological questions embedded in the event presented

- An identification of the cultural dynamics

- An identification of the personal dynamics

- Reflections on the key issues and dynamics regarding a pastoral response to the event (course syllabus)

The leader then reviews this feedback on the incident and uses it in writing a fully developed theological reflection case study, which he or she posts on the Web. This practice develops the skill of doing theological reflection, improves the quality of the final theological case studies, and provides the field education director with greater access to the experiences of intern students. The process also models a resource for doing communal theological reflection in the midst of full-time ministries with colleagues who may be widely dispersed.

While this use of Web-based technology for supporting the community of student interns does not replace the formative role of colleagues meeting face-to-face, it certainly bridges the barriers of time and distance. It may also encourage the prospect of forming online wisdom communities of experienced pastoral ministers who, immersed in various ministries and working in different locales, nevertheless want to engage in a regular process of communal theological reflection with colleagues.

Forming Master Preachers as an Online Wisdom Community

The task of forming new preachers and updating those currently in the preaching ministry ranks as one of theological education's most urgent priorities today. Web-based technology in Aquinas Institute's doctor of ministry in preaching degree program provides a way to aid this important task. The faculty designed this degree program to include two core homiletic seminars, taught as the third and the sixth courses of the six-course core curriculum. The core seminar begins with seven weeks of online instruction followed by a five-day, face-to-face intensive on the home campus, and concludes with eight more weeks online. One of the objectives of the course is to "self-critically and collegially seek greater simplicity, harmony, and brilliance in the praxis of preaching" (course syllabus). The course includes readings on homiletic method and theory as well as mutual critique of three preachings.

If formation in preaching was something of a solitary activity in the past—stressing, perhaps, the mechanics of the homily and the development of certain communication skills—the pedagogy in this course stresses a critical, theoretical, and collegial approach. The students, who regularly preach at ministries located throughout the country and internationally, follow a highly developed method for presenting homilies and homily case studies when the group meets in intensive sessions on campus. Web-based technology, however, allows them to present and critique each other's homilies from a distance. Using readily available technologies, participants record, digitize, and then post preaching events on the course website.[23] They also post a companion case study for each preaching event that includes: an analysis of the congregation, the hermeneutic approach used to interpret the biblical text, the preacher's homiletic approach, the preacher's goals, the text of the preaching, and the preacher's reflections on the event. Working in small groups, students use the threaded discussion board to review and share their critiques or each other's preaching events and case studies. For each online preaching presentation, the members of the preachers' wisdom community follow a structured process of critical reflection. Using the written case study, they examine the preacher's analysis of the congregation, biblical hermeneutics, learning goals, and the homiletic form and approach; they listen carefully to the preaching event itself; and they review the reflection offered by the preacher's local feedback group. With that preparation, participants in the seminar would receive the following assignment:

1. If there were any points in the preaching where you felt lost or confused, describe these as carefully as possible.

2. Analyze the homily, with attention given first to theological and biblical content and then to the style of preaching, addressing both strengths and possible goals for future growth.

3. How did this preaching meet the learning goals established by the preacher in the case study?

The use of the Web allows for clear presentations of preaching events, and the structured online group work facilitates detailed and constructive peer critique. It also cultivates a collegial experience of learning for this wisdom community of emerging master preachers, many of whom are diocesan priests.

The Pedagogy of the Online Wisdom Community: New Insights

The thesis of this chapter is that online teaching can be especially effective in pedagogical design as a way of cultivating wisdom communities for critical theological reflection. The rapport or immediacy established in the classroom can be extended in the virtual environment as students and instructors work online. The lessons learned by the Aquinas faculty in its use of Web-based teaching can be instructive.

First, Web-based teaching is most appropriately used to further the learning of students and instructors working face-to-face. The effectiveness of instructional technology builds on the quality of relationships developed among students and instructor as they work together in real time. The energy, creativity, and openness of learners working together can be transferred into a virtual context only if it is first established in real time.

Second, a careful use of Web-based teaching can deepen and intensify the learner's critical encounter with the deep mysteries of faith. The power of language to lay bare the transcendent in everyday life, described by Sandra Schneiders in her discussion of scriptural metaphor and symbol,[24] is often operative in online conversations of learners who have developed trusting relationships and are deeply committed to the process of transformative learning. This counters the claim that technology inevitably isolates its users, that it depersonalizes the learning experience, and thus is inappropriate for theological reflection.

Third, online teaching and learning offers unique features that encourage interactivity among learners.[25] This can be seen, for example, in the structure of a typical threaded discussion. The expectation that everyone needs to contribute to the discussion question is a decided gain when one thinks of the typical classroom and the tendency of some students to dominate while others "hide." More introverted students in particular find the flow of an asynchronous discussion board congenial to their preferred style of learning, for it allows them time and space to reflect and formulate their written response. Further, the design of the Web discussion board focuses on the theological question at hand, not a particular individual. It addresses a question to all the participants. The dialogue that ensues is not simply a dialogue between the instructor and individual students, as is sometimes the case in the face-to-face dynamics of the classroom. Nor does the theological conversation occur only through the instructor. He or she can "step aside" in the online format, remaining present to the process while allowing the students to take the lead. This simple fact makes a world of difference. Students in online groups find themselves in charge, mutually responsible for their learning, and accountable to each other. The interactive structure of the Web format encourages students to engage in learning as a cooperative venture.

Fourth, through the Web, students benefit from the opportunity to do theological reflection in community. The "expandable" character of virtual reality offers space where various groups of learners can meet. Practitioners in pastoral ministry, fellow students from different cultural contexts, and theological experts can be invited to join a wisdom community setting. An ever-widening sense of community enriches the work of theological reflection and offers a host of creative possibilities.

Finally, like any other teaching strategy, the use of technology can prove ineffective in teaching and learning. It is one thing to expound on one's pedagogical principles and quite another to learn to use technology well. Instructional technologists talk about the hazards of the "last mile connectivity," a reference to the fact that the best communications infrastructure in the world is useless if insufficient attention has been paid to connecting it to individual homes and businesses. Similarly, the use of technology in theological pedagogy will prove effective only if faculty are willing to listen and patiently work with each other, sharing their mistakes as well as their successes, retaining a sense of humor and encouraging the spirit of innovation.

Technology and Institutional Planning: A "Bricks and Clicks" Approach

What insights might the experience of Aquinas Institute faculty with Web-based teaching offer to the wider mission of theological education today? How might theological educators—including boards of trustees, seminary administrators, and faculty members—understand technology as a resource for teaching and learning? This section describes a hybrid model for using technology in teaching and learning that combines Web-based learning and traditional classroom interaction.[26]

One proponent of a hybrid approach to the use of technology in higher education is Van Weigel, professor of ethics and economic development at Eastern College.[27] Higher education today, he notes, typically views the usefulness of instructional technology in terms of accessibility and marketing (p. 43). Many schools in recent years have created online distance education programs with the hope of reaching more students at a greater distance from campus and at lower costs.[28] Technology's use as an instrument for promoting depth or quality in teaching and learning, however, is often overlooked. He writes: "The distance education solution has been advanced as the means to accommodate the projected growth in student enrollments or extend the geographic reach of the marketplace for students. The fact that Internet technologies can simultaneously improve both the accessibility and the quality of educational experiences is rarely emphasized" (p. 43). In light of this, Weigel proposes a hybrid model, emphasizing depth as well as access, blending the best of traditional on-campus teaching and learning with online or technologically mediated resources.

In Weigel's model, technology should be designed around the pedagogical goal of developing what he calls "deep learning." Deep learning, he says, "promotes the development of conditionalized knowledge and metacognition through communities of inquiry" (p. 5). Conditionalized knowledge is "knowledge that specifies the contexts in which it is useful and recognizes its own limitations. Students gain conditionalized knowledge only when they have the opportunity to apply disciplinary concepts and methodologies to varied contexts and knowledge domains" (p. 5). Surface knowledge, far more common in higher education, is instruction that is content with textbook descriptions and applications of concepts, but that offers little chance for learners to explore their own experiences and questions (p. 5). Metacognition is "the ability to think about thinking—the art of thinking" (p. 7). Weigel notes that metacognition develops both an awareness of oneself as a learner and the capacity to manage our own development as learners (p. 7).

Conditionalized knowledge and metacognition come together most effectively in communities of practice, or "communities of inquiry" (p. 7). People learn only by interacting with others in particular communities of thought, values, and beliefs. Such communal learning should aim, ultimately, at something that endures: the cultivation of wisdom. Weigel writes:

> Higher education can have no higher calling than to create learning environments that inspire wonder. Wisdom cannot be programmed into a curriculum or delivered as an educational outcome. But it is possible to create learning communities that are conducive to wisdom. Such "wisdom-friendly" learning environments would provide students with many opportunities to reflect on how the possession of knowledge creates new responsibilities to use it well. The ancient truth that knowledge imparts responsibility—"to whom much is given, of him will much be required" (Luke 12:48) —could not have greater relevance in the classrooms of our day (p. 140).

It is at the service of such depth education that Weigel views the role of technology in pedagogy. The Web is, by design, a place of connection and interaction. Moreover, the growing availability of broadband Internet access makes it increasingly reliable and cost effective to a growing number of students. "Although there is no intrinsic connection between deep learning and e-learning," Weigel writes, "the two are intertwined. . . . From a practical standpoint, deep learning and e-learning are inseparable. It is simply not possible to provide a broad cross section of students with depth educational curricula unless Internet technologies are used" (p. 5). From a pedagogical perspective, the future of higher education will increasingly call for a "bricks and clicks" (p. 23) approach, combining the best of face-to-face instruction with the resources that Internet technologies now make available:

> Depth education is a hybrid or blended approach to e-learning that combines the best features of the brick-and-mortar classroom with virtual environments. In contrast to approaches that use e-learning technologies as another delivery system for traditional education, depth education can be implemented in a holistic fashion across the disciplinary span of college and university curricula, thereby placing e-learning at the core of the curriculum.[29]

The ideal of depth education offers seminary boards, administrators, and faculties a useful paradigm out of which to think of technology for theological teaching and learning. "Conditionalized knowledge," "metacognition," and "communities of inquiry" are equally characteristics of good theological pedagogy. Good theological teaching and learning aims at helping students faithfully and critically appropriate the Christian tradition. Theological inquiry attempts to make working sense of the great Christian mysteries, aware of the various contexts and cultural settings in which we engage those mysteries. Theological pedagogy is also attentive to issues of hermeneutics and method, helping students learn how to think theologically as they minister. Such inquiry is always a communal endeavor, for to theologize is to enter into a conversation on issues that precede us and endure beyond us. Theological teaching and learning demands the kinds of critical, intentional, and wisdom friendly learning environments that Weigel describes as depth education.

The hybrid "bricks and clicks" approach that Weigel proposes has value for those seeking to understand the role of technology as a resource for theological education. In focusing on the quality of teaching and learning, the hybrid approach challenges the view that technology is important for research, communications, and marketing, but not necessarily for the classroom. The hybrid approach also challenges the distorted view that theologians have to become experts to use technology well or that a school needs a full-blown commitment to distance education in order to benefit from a well-thought-out technology program. The "bricks and clicks" model invites theological educators to explore ways in which technology might serve as a resource for cultivating greater depth throughout the entire curriculum, whether for residential programs or distance education offerings. The experience of Aquinas Institute suggests some possibilities in this regard. Blending the best of on-campus learning with carefully developed Web activities offers all theological schools a valuable way in which to envision the potential use of technology in theological teaching and learning.

Technology and the Challenges Facing Theological Education Today

Theological educators assessing the role of technology as a resource for teaching and learning must be particularly mindful today of the challenges of diversity, integration, and assessment discussed earlier in this book. As the authors have shown, these issues are extremely complex. The practical value of technology will depend in part on its usefulness in helping theologians creatively respond to the range of diversity in the classroom, while also offering new opportunities for integrative learning and assessment. In this final section I would like to present a series of questions and reflections that a faculty member might ponder in designing a hybrid course that uses Web-based instruction. These reflections are not intended to be exhaustive nor geared just to issues of technology in teaching. Indeed, the questions and reflections reflect what any good teacher would ponder in developing a course plan.

Technology and the Challenges of Diversity

Katarina Schuth has researched and described the kinds of cultural, generational, family-of-origin, and theological differences that characterize the seminarians and lay students in our classrooms.[30] Students also differ greatly in the academic backgrounds they bring to the seminary, particularly in the areas of philosophy, critical thinking, the humanities, and in the ability to do graduate-level research and writing. Given this growing diversity in our seminary populations, the instructor preparing to teach will want to ask certain questions as he or she designs the course syllabus.

Who are the students that I am teaching? How are they like and unlike me? The seminarian and lay student profiles presented in chapter 1 reveal the kinds of diversity typically found in today's theological classroom. Questions of identity explored in the early days of any course need to go beyond superficial introductions. My practice is to create a discussion board on the course website that specifically invites people to introduce themselves to each other in some depth, so that both instructor and students can become acquainted with the rich diversity in cultural background, gender, and life experiences that students typically bring.

What are the essential learning skills needed for students to be successful in this course? These should be spelled out in the course syllabus with attention to providing resources for students who have remedial needs. The course website can alert students to online programs, websites, multimedia presentations, and other resources that are of special interest or help. Most faculties already post on their school's websites a list of online instructional aids (see, for example, http://www.ai.edu/life/index.html) to assist students with particular learning skills. Developing such resources is helpful because the good work of one instructor can easily become available to an entire school community.

What is my preferred teaching style and does it encourage interactivity in the classroom? Teaching and learning are more than simply the transfer of information; they form cooperative activity. This needs to be modeled in the classroom. By developing an environment of interactivity in the classroom, the instructor better equips students to "extend" this style of learning to the Web. This issue is critical in using a hybrid mode. If interactive dynamics are not part of classroom work, it is unlikely they will be present in Web assignments.

How do I make the experience of diversity an opportunity for learning in the classroom? Clearly not all the diversity experienced in the classroom is helpful. There are basic issues of academic prerequisites, logic, and critical thinking skills, and formational issues around openness to learning that need to be addressed elsewhere. Professors today may still quietly bemoan the fact that seminary students are not "what they were in my time." Yet the diversity that we see reflected in our seminary classrooms mirrors the increasingly globalized world in which we live. In the church and in our classrooms this calls for a new appreciation of what it means to be "catholic" and a deeper commitment to growth in the skills of intercultural communication.[31] While Web-based teaching and learning appears ideally suited for homogeneous groups, it can also be used to promote learning among heterogeneous groups.[32]

It is possible, in fact, to design online learning to leverage the differences that exist among students by intentionally creating diverse working groups within a course. This calls for training in online communication skills, the development of course learning covenants, and ongoing discussion of the impact that social and ecclesial location, gender, and hermeneutical approaches have on interpretation. The formation of diverse online groups may also require training in the "how to" of theological dialogue, for example using the principles of the Catholic Common Ground Initiative.[33] The structure of online learning and its usefulness in structuring small group work can be an effective tool in which to introduce learners to diverse theological and cultural worldviews.

Technology and the Challenges of Integration

Theological learning demands strategies for integration. According to the accreditation standards of the Association of Theological Schools, learning is a multifaceted activity involving critical thinking, the acquisition of knowledge, the ability to do research and to engage in scholarly discourse, the ability to understand and access one's tradition and its identity, and the development of that ministerial and spiritual maturity expected of the church's ministers.[34] Such a comprehensive view of learning is, indeed, a life-long task. How can technology be used to facilitate this process of integrative learning?

One pedagogical option lies in envisioning the Web as a means by which learners can gain access to important and interesting "communities of practice" within the Christian tradition. John Seeley Brown and Paul Duguid observe that learning is more than simply acquiring and digesting sums of information. Effective learning requires becoming an "insider," gaining access to distinct communities and their ways of thinking and valuing.[35] They write:

> Indeed, knowing only the explicit—mouthing the formulas or the plays—is often exactly what gives the outsider away. Insiders know more. By coming to inhabit the relevant community, they get to know not just what the standard answers are, but the real questions and why they matter. . . . Learning involves inhabiting the streets of a community's culture. The community may include astrophysicists, architects, or acupuncturists, but learning involves experiencing its cultural peculiarities.[36]

Integrative learning is always, at root, a process of inculturation, of engaging and being engaged by differing ways of living and understanding the Christian faith. For theological educators, the challenge of integration consists in helping students access those multiple communities of thought and practice where the wisdom of the tradition is being lived out in wise and pastorally effective ways.

The Web's ability to host in virtual time and space a variety of communities of practice makes it an important resource for integrative learning. A school can use the Web as a communications tool to help students encounter a range of important thinkers and pastoral issues: for example, a lecture given by an African bishop deeply involved in his country's HIV/AIDS crisis, a colloquium with area business leaders on professional ethics, a monthly interreligious dialogue that includes members of the local Islamic community, or a day of prayer on Dominican spirituality. For instructors, the Web can be used to help students encounter new ways of thinking and practicing the faith and thus serve as a tool for integrative learning.

The Web can also encourage integration by allowing groups of students to form communities of practice as one of the learning strategies of a course. The use of a course website creates a flexible structure in virtual time where students can further refine a topic of interest, assemble and research the available bibliographical sources, engage in ongoing discussion on what they are learning, and produce a common project that reflects their "insider" knowledge of their study.

Most significantly, the virtual nature of the Web allows a community of practice to include people far outside the classroom. Pastors and denominational leaders and specialists in the everyday work of pastoral care can be invited in or students studying on one continent can be in constructive dialogue with students and experts on another continent. In any number of ways, virtual space can help students link their intellectual knowledge with life in the church tradition and society around them. Recently a student analyzing Roman Catholic documents on ecumenism decided to do so from the perspective of her virtual presence to the people and churches of Northern Ireland. Through personal contacts and a host of Web resources, she was able to present, in a very effective way, the challenge of ecumenism in a country where religious differences are often a matter of life and death. Through the Web she participated in a community far away from her own context; through the use of multimedia technology, the class benefited from her attempts to integrate this issue.

Technology and the Challenges of Classroom Assessment

One of the most challenging aspects of teaching and learning is out-comes assessment, which includes the evaluation of student classroom performance. It remains the case for instructors who use technology for course delivery. How, for example, does an instructor grade student compositions when they are in the form of weekly postings on a threaded discussion board? In a hybrid course, what weight does an instructor place on student online work in relation to the learning activities that take place in the face-to-face setting of the classroom? How does an instructor establish an assessment plan that adequately relates the use of technology to the particular goals of a given course? These kinds of questions are very much in play as theological faculties implement new forms of technology for teaching.

Weigel advocates an approach to course assessment that he calls "embedded evaluation."[37] The use of the Web to engage students in small group projects provides an online context wherein an instructor can give regular input to students, encourage students to offer con-structive feedback to each other, and invite learners to reflect on the process and quality of their own learning.[38] There is a certain trans-parency or public character about Web interaction that makes learner performance easier to evaluate. Pallof and Pratt describe their own approach to online embedded course evaluation:

> In the spirit of collaboration and reflection, evaluation of student progress should not fall to the instructor alone. Students should be encouraged to comment on one another's work, and self-evaluation should be embedded in the final performance evaluation of each student. As the course progresses, we ask that students provide feed-back to one another on assignments. In addition, at the end of a term we request that students send us a private e-mail with a descriptive evaluation of the performance of their student colleagues as well as their own performance. We use this feedback along with quality and quantity of participation and performance on assignments and in discussions as measures of overall student performance.[39]

This kind of embedded assessment strategy seems significantly richer than a summative approach that depends solely on a final examination or research paper for the course grade.

In this approach to assessment, the instructor accompanies the students online, intervening at points to encourage or challenge. The presence of the instructor can model the kind of responsible interactivity that he or she expects. One of the challenges for instructors in this model of assessment is "remaining with" the learners as the course unfolds, replying to their work in a timely manner, and offering the kind of patient and constructive feedback that students are able to hear. Experience shows that if students are to value their time on the Web, they need a clear understanding of how those learning activities are being assessed by the instructor. Undoubtedly, theological educators will need to work together to develop more robust assessment strategies that take full advantage of the Web and the virtual learning community as a context for ongoing and formative course evaluation.

Conclusion

The future shape of instructional technology in theological teaching and learning is only beginning to unfold. We are at the start of a long process of discovering new ways that technology can be used in the service of good pedagogy. Web-based technologies, however, can significantly contribute to theological teaching and learning by extending our access to knowledge and resources. More importantly, they can help form communities of learning and practice—wisdom communities—where the richness of the tradition in conversation with culture can be appropriated to meet the challenges of our time.

Using Technology in the Wider Church Today

The experience of theological educators shows how the Web can be used to complement and build upon traditional strategies of gathering people into face-to-face settings for teaching and learning. How might technology be used by parishes, dioceses, and other communities to meet the needs of the church on the local level? The needs for teaching and training on the local level are unique and urgent. The following are only a few of the ways the Web might be used at the parish and diocesan levels:

– A parish adult education program designed around regular gatherings at the parish center and ongoing, interactive faith sharing on the Web.

– A parish synod designed to include plenary sessions at the parish along with a series of structured, small group discussions carried on over a period of time on the Web.

- A parish online preaching ministry, where young people, women, married men, and others among the nonordained are invited to offer a reflection on the Sunday Scripture text, which is made available to the wider community on the Web.

- A diocesan program of academic and pastoral formation, tailored to the needs of the learners and the local church, designed to include face-to-face intensive sessions as well as ongoing reading and discussion sessions on the Web.

- A program of ongoing professional development for parish staffs, in areas of theology, spirituality, and leadership training, drawing on expert resources from throughout the country, which is available in whole or in part on the Web.

- A library of selected Catholic literature, including classics as well as contemporary magisterial and theological writings, with opportunities for small group discussion, available on the Web.

NOTES

1. The Wabash Center for Teaching and Learning in Theology and Religion helped coordinate this Lilly initiative. For a list of participating theological institutions see "Information Technology for Theological Teaching Grants," Wabash Center for Teaching and Learning in Theology and Religion, http://www.wabashcenter.wabash.edu/infotechnology/index.html and http://www.wabashcenter.wabash.edu/infotechnology/infotech2.html.

2. Raymond Williams, "Information Technology in Seminaries: Getting Technical," *Christian Century* (February 7–14, 2001) 14–17; Paul Soukup, S.J., Francis J. Buckley, S.J., David Robinson, S.J., "The Influence of Information Technologies on Theology," *Theological Studies* 62 (2001) 366–77.

3. Peter Hodgson, *God's Wisdom: Toward a Theology of Education* (Louisville: Westminster, 1999) 87–124.

4. Walter Burghardt, "This World Desperately Needs Theologians," *Catholic Mind* (March 1981) 36.

5. Lois Malcolm, "Teaching as Cultivating Wisdom for a Complex World," in *The Scope of Our Art: The Vocation of the Theological Teacher*, eds. L. Gregory Jones and Stephanie Paulsell (Grand Rapids, Mich.: Eerdsmans, 2002) 154.

6. David Kelsey has critiqued the use of electronically mediated forms of "distance learning" on basic principles of Christian theological anthropology. He explicitly questions the theological appropriateness of using technology in theological schooling. See "Spiritual Machines, Personal Bodies, and God: Theological Education and Theological Anthropology," _Teaching Theology and Religion_ (2002) 2–9.

7. Elizabeth Patterson, "The Questions of Distance Education," _Theological Education_ (1996) 68–69.

8. On theological pedagogy and the use of technology, see the following: Scott Cormode, "Using Computers in Theological Education: Rules of Thumb," _Theological Education_ (1999) 101–15; Richard Ascough, "Designing Online Distance Education," _Teaching Theology and Religion_ (2002) 17–29; and Mary E. Hess "Pedagogy and Theology in Cyberspace: 'All that We Can't Leave Behind . . .,'" _Teaching Theology and Religion_ (2002) 30–38.

9. Rena M. Pallof and Keith Pratt, _Lessons from the Cyberspace Classroom: The Realities of On-line Teaching_ (San Francisco: Jossey-Bass, 2001) 153.

10. Ibid., 154.

11. Ibid.

12. Williams, _Getting Technical_, 17.

13. For an overview of the goals and course content of the distance education MAPM degree, see "Distance Learning Master of Arts in Pastoral Ministry," Aquinas Institute of Theology, http://www.ai.edu/programs/academic/mapm/index.html.

14. I am indebted to my faculty colleagues at the Aquinas Institute who designed and embody these principles.

15. Mary Margaret Pazdan, "Wisdom Communities: Models for Christian Formation and Pedagogy," _Theological Education_ (1998) 25–30.

16. Ibid., 25.

17. Ibid., 26.

18. Here I understand "theological reflection," in a broad sense, to refer to critical theological inquiry as it is carried out in the various theological disciplines, each of which employs different hermeneutical approaches. Roger Haight notes that, in a general way, all theological interpretation is necessarily governed by three criteria: faithfulness to the Scriptures and the central Christian doctrines, intelligibility within a given context, and empowerment of Christian life. See his _Dynamics of Theology_ (Maryknoll, N.Y.: Orbis, 2001) 210–12. I take his suggestion as a starting point; each subdiscipline

within theology will further specify the structure of critical theological reflection within the context of the object of its study.

19. The threaded discussion board is a forum on the course website where students can log on and post messages. Structurally, it is similar to e-mail except that more than one student can be registered to the same discussion forum. Richard Ascough describes the meaning of the phrase "threaded discussion" this way: "Threading refers to messages that concern the same topic and have the same topic line. A single thread lists all messages for that subject in a format in which replies are indented to show responses to the original message. Separate topics are discussed as separate threads. This helps organize discussions and allows for ease of navigation through a particular subject." See Ascough, *Designing for Online Distance Education*, 23.

20. The structure of the online discussion questions presented here is based on Pazdan's insight into the style of interactive learning characteristic of the wisdom community. See Pazdan, *Wisdom Communities*, 26–28.

21. Mary Margaret Pazdan, "Hermeneutical and Pedagogical Challenges," *Proceedings of the Central States Regional Meeting of the Society of Biblical Literature and the American Schools of Oriental Research* (2000) 108–09.

22. Ascough, *Designing for Online Distance Education*, 23.

23. Among such technologies are Qualcomm's PureVoice (http://www.cdmatech.com/solutions/products/purevoice.jsp) and RealOne Player (http://www.real.com/), and videotapes or digital video compact disks.

24. Internet technologies continue to perfect the delivery of stunning graphics and streaming audio and visual images. Yet language is still our most essential tool in the communication of truth and values. Schneiders writes: "Language is our highest form of symbol making as well as our most refined instrument of interpretation. It is the medium of both understanding and expression, and therefore it is not surprising that we metaphorically attribute speech to anything we experience as symbolic." Sandra Schneiders, *The Revelatory Text* (Collegeville: Liturgical Press, 1999) 37.

25. There is abundant literature available on the related topics of virtual community and learner interactivity. A helpful treatment of these themes can be found in Rena Pallof and Keith Pratt, *Building Learning Communities in Cyberspace* (San Francisco: Jossey-Bass, 1999) as well as their *Lessons from the Cyberspace Classroom*.

26. On hybrid teaching, see W. Sean Chamberlin, "Face-to-Face vs. Cyberspace: Finding the Middle Ground," *Syllabus*, http://www.syllabus.com/article.asp?id=5857; William H. Riffee, "Putting a Faculty Face on Distance Education Programs," *Syllabus*, http://www.syllabus.com/article.asp?id=7233;

and David G. Brown, "Hybrid Courses Are Best," *Syllabus,* http://www.syllabus.com/article.asp?id=4582.

27. Van B. Weigel, *Deep Learning for a Digital Age: Technology's Untapped Potential to Enrich Higher Education* (San Francisco: Jossey-Bass, 2002). Unless otherwise noted, references to Weigel are cited in the text by the page number.

28. According to Weigel, most of these programs are neither cost-effective nor pedagogically sound. Far too often courses are simply "packaged" for online use, leading to what he calls a "commoditization" of instruction. Weigel, *Deep Learning,* 35–39.

29. Ibid., 23. Weigel offers a concrete description of how he uses the Web as part of a hybrid teaching approach. See chapters 3 and 4 of *Deep Learning,* 60–126.

30. Katarina Schuth, O.S.F., *Seminaries, Theologates, and the Future of Church Ministry: An Analysis of Trends and Transitions* (Collegeville: Liturgical Press, 1999) 66–94. The impact of diversity can also be seen among the ranks of those currently ordained or working as full-time lay ecclesial ministers in the Catholic church. See Dean Hoge and Jacqueline Wenger, *Evolving Visions of the Priesthood* (Collegeville: Liturgical Press, 2003).

31. Robert Schreiter, writing on the impact of globalization on cultural life and the church's mission, suggests the need for a rethinking of the ancient mark of the church as "catholic." He writes: "A new catholicity, then, is marked by a wholeness of inclusion and fullness of faith in a pattern of intercultural exchange and communication. . . . A new catholicity can meet the challenges of our time, both as a theological vision of the Church and as a policy for intercultural communication." Robert Schreiter, *The New Catholicity: Theology between the Global and the Local* (Maryknoll, N.Y.: Orbis, 1999) 132–33.

32. Some educators warn that technology inevitably tends to minimize diversity in the educational process. Elizabeth Patterson, for example, writes: "One of the more troubling elements in distance study is that it comes at a time when theological education has an almost unanimous commitment toward the necessity of incorporating diversity as a foundational value. Such diversity has tremendous potential for enriching learning, but in distance education, where the learner is dependent on packaged course materials, students may not have access to much diversity." Patterson, "The Questions of Distance Education," 67. This need not be so, however. Pedagogy, informed by the ideal of catholicity as Schreiter describes it, will be attentive to diversity and intercultural communication and reflect that in the ways technology is used in course design.

33. *Called to Be Catholic: Church in a Time of Peril,* statement prepared by the National Pastoral Life Center (New York, August 12, 1996).

34. Association of Theological Schools, "General Institutional Standards: Learning, Teaching, and Research: Theological Scholarship, no. 3.1.1.," *Bulletin* (1998) 55.

35. John Seely Brown and Paul Duguid, "Universities in the Digital Age," *Change* 28 (1996), under "Colleges, Communities, and Learning," http://www2.parc.com/ops/members/brown/papers/university.html.

36. Ibid. See also Brown and Duguid, *The Social Life of Information* (Boston: Harvard Business School Press, 2000) 133–43.

37. Weigel, *Deep Learning,* 14.

38. Ibid., 14–15.

39. Pallof and Pratt, *Lessons from the Cyberspace Classroom,* 34.

CHAPTER 8

Leading Change:
A Reflection on Context, Principles, and Virtues

Jeanne McLean, Ph.D.
Donald Senior, C.P.

Introduction

The Keystone Conferences sought to generate significant institutional change by engaging teams of faculty and administrators to reflect on the task of strengthening "theological teaching for the Church's ministries." As a result of these collegial conversations, each team developed a project for its school that would have a long-term, positive impact on the quality of teaching and learning. Success, however, required more than enthusiasm and good ideas. The real challenge was to provide leadership within their communities that would inspire interest, engage broad-based participation, and cultivate community ownership of the project. The real challenge, in short, was to create an environment for change to occur.

Change is a constant factor in the life of most theological schools and can come from within or outside the institution and happen voluntarily or be forced by necessity. Whatever its source or reason, senior administrators bear particular responsibility for leading and managing change around the mission, curriculum and program development, faculty scholarship, or teaching and learning. How the president/rector and the chief academic officer understand their leadership roles relative to each other and to the board and faculty, and how attentive they are to the *context* for change and the *process* of change, can determine the impact that change has on institutional life. It is clear that the *methods* used to promote change are often as important for their organizations as the change itself.

The Communal Context for Change

In view of the current challenges to theological education, schools are constantly faced with ongoing adaptation and change in order to remain viable. Leadership has an obviously key role in helping institutions do the hard work of adaptation but exercises that role within a particular institutional environment or "culture." What institutional factors does leadership need to keep in mind to help facilitate adaptation or change?

1. *Leadership should engage the entire community in a process of thinking through the mission of the institution.*

The primary purpose of leadership within an educational institution is to insure an environment in which the vital work of teaching and learning can thrive. As a result, school leaders have the responsibility from time to time and at key turning points in the school's life to bring the overall picture of the school's life into focus, to keep in view the varying constituent parts of the whole, and to lift up the mission of the school for communal consideration. This may be the case, for example, when considering a substantial new program or when facing the possibility of budget cuts. At moments like these, effective leadership assists the school to reflect on its essential mission as it considers how individual initiatives relate to that overall mission, and how that mission can be revitalized in the face of environmental changes in the wider world.

Several years ago the Association of Theological Schools challenged faculty and administrators to think about the "vocation" of a theology school. Vocation in this sense was not applied to the individual but to the corporate vocation of the institution. What is the guiding purpose of this institution? What was its original inspiration and how did it evolve over time? How well do the individual components cohere around this fundamental vocation?

Such questions posed in a thoughtful and constructive manner help an academic community do the work of adaptive change. All effective leaders recognize the importance of strategic planning. Giving attention to one's corporate mission and thinking it through together should be a vital and ongoing component of any organizational planning.

2. *Leadership should be attuned to those key outside "voices" or wider environmental factors that compel change on the part of an institution.*

Effective change and adaptation will not take place solely because key leaders within the institution decide it should happen. Often the impulse for change will come from "outside voices" or factors that force their way into a school's consciousness. Because presidents, deans, and other administrators work more on the outside boundaries of their institutions—dealing with trustees, donors, church officials, vendors, and the wider public—they can serve as "sentries" alert to the winds of change and able to interpret their significance for the school's mission. Many schools of theology have found themselves changing due to these "outside factors": the influx of laymen and women seeking spiritual enrichment in graduate theology courses; the perspectives of business and marketing represented by trustees; the pastoral perspectives of church officials, pastoral ministers, or people in the pew. A few years ago in a faculty assembly one professor who was wary of the nontraditional students beginning to appear in his classroom referred to them as "street people." Now such "street people" are a majority of the student body at his institution and have brought changes to the schedule and content of the curriculum.

Seminaries and schools of theology, of course, need to exercise prudent discernment in evaluating the impact of all outside factors. At the same time, we can also think of such impulses for change as being responsive to the needs of the Church and the world. Modern missiologists speak of "mission in reverse." This means that the tradition of bringing the Gospel to those who have never experienced it is reframed to recognize the reality that the Spirit is already at work in the wider world. Those with a mission, then, receive as well as give in relation to the people they serve.

3. *Effective leadership needs to be alert to the self-interest of key groups within the institution and realize the "organic" nature of institutions when proposing change or adaptation.*

Anyone who has served in a leadership capacity soon learns that institutions have lives of their own. Initiatives, no matter how seemingly brilliant or valuable, that are not well received by the key people within an institution who make things work will eventually be stopped in their tracks by inertia or disinterest. Effective change occurs to the degree that key people at all levels within the institution perceive that what is proposed is advantageous and meaningful (even if not welcome or entirely comfortable). If they don't perceive it this way, no matter how urgent and cogent the project may seem to those in leadership, very little will happen long term.

When considering change or adaptation, it is also helpful to think of an institution in organic rather than architectural or static terms. Like most institutions, the inner workings of an academic institution do not operate with gears and levers but as an organic reality. New initiatives cannot simply be built one on top of the other or by simply adding or rearranging vital parts as if one were building an inert structure. Rather, change within an institution formed of human beings has its own dynamism and energy levels that either welcome change or resist it. Thus change will not be effective unless there is readiness to accept change. Nor should new change wait until all previous initiatives are complete and settled as if one were building one floor of a structure on top of another. As organic entities, vital institutions need new initiatives and the prospect of change to fuel their inner life and to keep people energized about the mission of an institution.

In concert with his or her colleagues, the savvy leader understands and accepts this organic and dynamic character of institutions and works in harmony with it. Patience and good timing determine when new projects should be proposed or when taking a deep breath is more appropriate.

4. *Effective leaders should assist their communities to develop the spiritual discipline needed to accept and utilize unwelcome realities.*

Profound change in an institution is often linked to adversity. Financial crises, unexpected personnel changes, and the intrusion of outside circumstances can all overturn months or years of careful planning and deflate the morale of an institution. Surely the recent crisis over sexual misconduct on the part of some priests and bishops and the questions posed about how church leaders responded to such behavior ranks as one of the most "unwelcome realities" the Church and the theological education community have faced in generations.

Yet it is often in circumstances like these that real and constructive change can take place. Facing such unwelcome and unexpected adverse circumstances requires collective spiritual discipline on the part of an institution. Can a community summon up the courage, the energy, and the imagination to deal with the unwelcome realities and turn them into opportunities for new life? Here again leadership plays a vital role in helping an institution collectively interpret such moments in a way that opens the possibility for new life to gain ground. One might think of this as a kind of "spiritual jujitsu" in which the negative force of an onrushing adversity is turned in a positive direction for the ultimate benefit of a community. What is at stake here is not some kind of organizational manipulation or technique but the capacity to evoke the values and strengths of our faith in confronting collective suffering.

How leaders act and speak at times of crisis often play a significant role in enabling a community to absorb adversity and move forward constructively. For example, social commentators acknowledged the leadership of Mayor Guiliani at a time of acute crisis for New York City by his presence and manner of speaking about an event of tragic proportions. His exercise of leadership contributed to renewing the hope and energy of a shaken community. Most seminary presidents and deans will not face tragedies of such magnitude, yet there are still significant moments of unwelcome realities in every community. The spirit in which leaders speak about such experiences and the way they convene and mobilize the key people in the institution can direct the energy of the institution toward new life.

In the case of the sexual misconduct crisis, for example, seminary presidents and deans could not afford to remain silent about this scandal. Many seminary leaders, in concert with their bishops or sponsoring religious communities, provided forums for faculty and students to share their reactions about the crisis. Many institutions took the occasion to review their own admissions policies and programs designed to help form students in priestly celibacy and healthy sexual development. Some schools also conducted public forums for their friends and donors, enabling the voice of the laity to be heard at this critical juncture in the church's life.

Taking such steps in a moment of crisis or suffering is an act of leadership, often requiring unusual courage. But in so doing leaders can enable an institution to face needed change in a more profound manner than when conditions are serene.

5. *Leaders need to be aware that while corporate planning is crucial for any institution, change also happens because of unexpected factors or opportunities or because someone (often but not always a leader) throws in a novel but compelling idea.*

Dealing with the unexpected can be disconcerting for anyone in leadership. A favorite axiom of many administrators is understandably,

"No surprises, please." There is the fear that we may not know how to cope with the unexpected or that it may take us into unfamiliar and uncharted waters. Surely the best route for introducing change is in the context of careful and well-prepared institutional planning. But often enough real change comes about because someone at the last minute proposes a compelling idea or a new opportunity suddenly lands on the doorstep. Readiness to respond and evaluate such surprises, rather than dismissing them, is an important component of good leadership. General Charles de Gaulle, whose unpredictability irritated allied strategic planners in World War II, also used the art of the surprise as a management "style" when he became President of the French Republic. He regularly threw his government colleagues into chaos by tossing provocative new ideas into the mix long after the planners had reached their conclusions.

The ability to absorb the unexpected can often be reflective of the leader's self-confidence. Rather than feeling one has to control the process and screen out surprises or be wary of new players in the mix, the leader who has the right kind of confidence is mission-directed and focused on the good of the institution as a whole. In that spirit new ideas or new actors that enter the stage unexpectedly may contribute to the institution's mission and thus can be seen as a source of new opportunities rather than as threats.

Principles for Leading Change

The study of chief academic officers in theological schools, on which this chapter draws, offers insight on ways faculty and administrators work together to effect change.[1] From that research and our own experience as administrators, we would highlight several guiding principles for leading the change process.

1. *Planning for change is most effective when the leadership team includes respected institutional leaders at every stage of the project who are drawn from the faculty and administration.*

In preparing for change, the president, dean, or project director should ask: Who are the people that need to be included, not just for their particular expertise, but for their credibility and positive influence on others? These are individuals who can work collaboratively and elicit the participation of others. Once identified, leadership needs to consider how these individuals could be most effectively brought into the process.

At one seminary, planning had begun on a new extension program that required off-site instruction and the use of technology for distance learning. The majority of faculty were not enthused. Aware that this initiative would meet with resistance, an experienced president and dean put faculty on the committee who could sell it to the faculty. The intent was not to stack the committee with strong supporters, but to have on the committee those who could work in a collegial and consultative manner to build support for the project. The president and dean understood that the composition of the working group would signal the importance of the project and ultimately secure the support, approval, and ownership of other members of the community.

2. *Effective change processes are broadly and genuinely consultative.*

While broad consultation tends to be highly valued by most schools, planning committees often neglect to consider at the outset who really needs to be consulted. They also need to identify how frequently and at what stages in the process consultation should occur in order to genuinely solicit fresh ideas and suggestions.

The failure to consult the right persons at the appropriate time can be devastating. The experience of curriculum revision in a Catholic seminary dramatically illustrates this point. In compliance with new denominational guidelines, the seminary faculty revised their pre-theology program so it would be a two-year rather than a one-year program. The faculty worked intensively over months to develop a two-year curriculum that received unanimous endorsement by administrators and faculty. It was only then that the president became concerned that many of the sponsoring bishops who regularly send students would not support the program. He asked the faculty to go back to the drawing board and start over. The decision to begin again was frustrating and demoralizing.

Another seminary had a similar experience in its effort to broaden program offerings to serve an increasingly diverse student body preparing for ministry in a multicultural church. The president, dean, and director of racial/ethnic studies at the school had worked with two local churches to establish an Hispanic Ministry Program. Throughout the process, they informed board members, alumni/ae, and faculty in related disciplines, and they achieved good collaboration with church leaders. When the proposal came forward for the vote of the entire faculty, however, it was defeated. Even the experienced administrators at this school had failed to address concerns about staffing and program quality with the faculty as a whole. The faculty was not appropriately consulted at a stage when their input would have been critical to the development of the program.

The timing of the consultation also can indicate its legitimacy and usefulness. Faculty and students are especially keen on detecting when consultation is legitimate and when it is *pro forma*. For consultation to be genuine, input has to be solicited at a formative stage in the process so that ideas received can be seriously considered by the committee for possible incorporation in the final product. The issue is including people at a stage in the process when their ideas can make a difference.

3. *Pacing the change process is critically important.*

In his book *Leadership without Easy Answers*, Ronald Heifetz considers it part of the leader's role to know if change is progressing at a rate that people can accept.[2] The leader must guide the process—from the initial discussions, through planning, to approving and implementing the decision. This insures a pace that allows enough time for consulting broadly, working through differences, and reaching agreement without losing momentum and draining people of enthusiasm and interest.

A problem with pacing can arise even when a planning process is otherwise sound. In one school, the dean of six years firmly believed one can never consult too much. When the school was seeking to move from a traditional five-day schedule to a four-day schedule of day and evening classes, the dean worked the better part of a year with all constituent groups to reach consensus. He worked with the executive committee of the faculty, held two student forums, brought the proposal to several faculty committees and academic divisions, and finally to the whole faculty. The difficulty came only at the end. The dean was pressured by the need to develop the schedule for the coming year before leaving on sabbatical. He needed a decision by March, so the pace accelerated. Although much consultation had occurred, the faculty felt rushed and the proposal seemed railroaded. The faculty voted to accept the proposal, but the change enjoyed little ownership and was not cheerfully implemented.

4. *Effective planning for change recognizes the value of informal consultation—the personal contacts made by the leaders of the project with other individuals and groups throughout the institution.*

One dean, who had been in his position for twelve years, frequently compared himself to Lyndon Baines Johnson. Like L.B.J., he firmly believed in winning the case in committees and having on the committees the strongest voices pro and con. The key to the dean's effectiveness, however, was that he supplemented committee work with frequent informal conversations with a broad range of faculty and other constituents in the hallways, in offices, and at social gatherings. Those who were particularly difficult to persuade were invited out for lunch or dinner. The value of this approach, he observed, is that one finds out what the roadblocks are so they can be addressed. More importantly, one comes to know the issues on people's minds and is able to build support one-on-one, one person at a time.

The deliberate use of this informal outreach underscores one of the most compelling findings of the study of academic deans—that leadership is rooted in personal relationships. Effective leaders are those who have strong professional relationships with their colleagues and, through those relationships, influence them to lend their support to worthy projects. That is why those identified as leaders within the community need to be directly involved and consulted. Approval and ownership of the change often depend upon it.

5. *All strategies for change must be tailored to the particular faculty and the distinctive institutional culture.*

Given the diversity of institutions, no single model of leadership or formula for effective change will work in every setting. In light of this, project leaders should reflect at the outset on what has worked and not worked in the past. Every school has those with a long institutional memory. One of the challenges in promoting change is to be informed by past practices while remaining open to consideration of new approaches that might be more effective.

The Distinctive Role of Positional Leaders

In addition to the guidelines discussed above, positional leaders like presidents and deans have additional opportunities and responsibilities for leading institutional change. No project will ultimately succeed without their strong and continued support. Each plays a distinct and significant role in achieving that success.

1. *Positional leaders have the responsibility to set the institutional agenda and to maintain community focus on projects of high priority.*

While various persons may share in the task of developing an institutional vision and goals, senior administrators are well positioned to elicit ideas and to articulate a coherent view of the school's direction. Even administrators strongly committed to working collegially find that their positions provide the distinctive opportunity to speak publicly and regularly on issues of community importance. As a result, they shape the discourse and define the priorities of the institution. Administrators often are surprised by the power of their office to direct the attention and energy of others to particular issues and to set the institutional agenda.

In the case of special initiatives, the president and dean can maintain community focus and momentum for a project by the priority they give it in working with faculty, students, and the board and by their explicit, public statements of support. Conversely, they also can subvert projects through their own inattention. Research has shown that successful projects often are attributed to positional leaders, not because they accomplished them single handedly or without the involvement and leadership of others, but because their active support was indispensable to keeping important projects alive within the community and ultimately to achieving common ownership of them.

2. *Effective leadership for change finds the right language to describe who we are and what we are doing as an institution.*

To motivate a religious institution for change and adaptation, effective leaders also face the challenge of finding the right language to describe the tasks that engage the community. Theological administrators and faculty understandably use the technical jargon of education and planning to describe what they are doing. At the same time, we should not forget who we are—a religious people with a profound and rich heritage of faith. Finding the appropriate and authentic language for the important tasks we do is itself an act of leadership. Such language should not be simply technical or bloodless but tap into the religious metaphors and deeper passions of our tradition. What are the gospel values, the biblical and theological images, and the motifs integral to our Catholic tradition that we want to appeal to as we consider the possibility of transformation within our institution? What are the basic convictions that sustain, unite, and inspire us at a level that rises above our corporate tensions? Tapping into these sources can bring new energy to a community.

Leaders can often have a profound influence on the choice of the right words to describe the identity and mission of an institution. Good leaders can refuse to be content with mere jargon or techno-speak either in official conversations within the institution or in communication with various publics. Obviously, such language cannot be merely sentimental or inappropriately homiletic. Linking the tasks of recruitment, curriculum revision, strategic planning, fiscal restructuring, or forging new initiatives to the profound metaphors and narratives of our biblical and theological heritage, reminds us who we are as people of faith and why we are investing in the enterprise of theological education on behalf of the Church. By bringing our religious tradition to bear on the work at hand, leaders become educators within their communities.

3. *Positional leaders are most successful in achieving lasting change when they elicit the broad participation and ownership of their communities.*

The study of academic leadership revealed that most academic officers actually had little *formal* authority or power to enact change. Their considerable potential for leadership came in subtler, often underestimated ways. Both presidents and deans considered that a primary privilege of their office—and an indispensable component of their leadership—was the ability to convene faculty and other constituents to give focused attention to important issues or projects. This privilege went beyond setting up committees and scheduling meetings. By virtue of their offices, they were able to initiate corporate conversations, to create occasions for extended community reflection, and to encourage discussion that would give projects priority and build institutional support and ownership for them.

Parker Palmer urges leaders to engage their communities in conversations about teaching and learning and offers practical advice on guiding such conversations.[3] Calling forth the community around issues of importance is indispensable to effective leadership. Palmer states:

> If we are to have communities of discourse about teaching and learning—communities that are intentional about the topics to be pursued and the ground rules to be practiced—we need leaders who can call people toward that vision. . . . Good talk about good teaching is unlikely to happen if presidents and provosts, deans and department chairs, do not *expect* and *invite* it into being on a regular basis. Those verbs are important because leaders who try to coerce conversation will fail. Conversation must be a free choice—but in the privatized academy, conversations begin only as leaders invite us out of our isolation into generative ways of using our freedom.[4]

Positional leaders in seminaries and schools of theology can raise up issues and invite colleagues to participate in conversations that will call them toward a corporate vision for their work as theological educators. There may be many different kinds of places—formal and informal, elegant and mundane—where these discussions take place. Effective leaders recognize the significant contribution such conversations can make to the project and to its support and ownership within the theological community.

Achieving broad community ownership for institutional initiatives through strategies such as these is a necessary component of effective leadership. As seasoned educators are fond of observing, "Deans and presidents come and go, but faculties remain." The ability of positional leadership to develop a broad-based commitment among various constituents of the school is essential for changes to endure. As effective leaders attest, a process that includes in-depth conversations and widespread consultation with faculty and other constituents affords the best assurance that institutional change will be significant and lasting.

4. Presidents and deans must educate the board of trustees about institutional needs and build relationships that foster collaboration and support.

Critical to the success of any major institutional initiative in a seminary or school of theology is the explicit support and ownership of the board of trustees. As representatives of the wider church and community, trustees can help maintain healthy external relationships and insure that the institution remains faithful to its mission. Trustees bring to the institution a certain critical distance from issues of change that can be emotionally charged for those inside the school community. They also foster good decision making by providing broader perspectives and experiences that complement the educational and ecclesial experience of presidents, deans, and faculty.

To carry out their responsibilities, trustees need to be adequately informed about the mission and internal operations of the institution. Presidents and deans play a critical role in developing an effective working relationship between board members and the other individuals and groups within the theological education community. In institutions committed to shared governance, presidents and deans are pivotal in insuring that all parties, particularly board members and faculty, understand their respective responsibilities and authority in governance.

Any significant change is an exercise in community building. The challenges discussed above and the principles that guide institutional leaders in meeting them apply in academic, pastoral, and civic communities alike. The importance of attending both to the communal *context* and to the collaborative *process* of change cannot be underestimated. The real test of leadership in promoting change is to get members of the community invested in its planning and implementation and, ultimately, to assume ownership of it.

Virtues for the Practice of Leadership

As leaders consider the challenge of helping their institutions face new realities and undertake the changes needed to adapt to them, they might remember some time-tested Christian virtues that go with this territory. Leaders (and their colleagues) need *humility*, that is, the kind of realism that prepares us for modest gains rather than spectacular triumphs. The advice that Dietrich Bonhoeffer gives to those who live in community seems apt here. He warns against "wish dreams," the ever-present liability of serious-minded Christians who bring with them "very definite ideas of what Christian life together should be and try to realize it."[5] The danger he notes is that such "wish dreamers" become disillusioned because they are more in love with their own idea of what community should be than they are with the actual community God gives them. Leaders, too, can fall into the trap of "wish dreams" about how their institutions should respond to their ideas and initiatives and end up wounded or embittered when the gains are much more modest.

A good dose of *tolerance* is a helpful virtue for leaders in the task of change. The decisions leaders make will not be welcome news to everyone, so a good leader cannot afford to have even subtle contempt for those who disagree with or oppose a course of action. Tolerance in this sense derives from a respect for the other members of the seminary community ultimately rooted in our understanding of the Church as the Body of Christ.

Finally, leaders need *perseverance,* which is another way of describing commitment to mission. In the wonderful phrase of Eugene Peterson, leaders and their institutions need to exercise "a long obedience in the same direction."[6] For most administrators, time is on their side in guiding an institution. Thoughtful and consistent action in accord with the true mission of an institution over time will bear good fruit. This might be considered a variant on the famous principle of Gamaliel who warned his fellow religious leaders about their opposition to the apostles, "If their purpose of activity is of human origin, it will destroy itself. If, on the other hand, it comes from God, you will not be able to destroy them. . . ." (Acts 5:38–39). Those who labor to prepare a new generation of religious leadership on behalf of the Church have every reason to believe that their work comes from God. In the big picture nothing will be able to destroy it. From that can come the confidence and serenity—as well as the humility—to embrace the challenge.

NOTES

1. This Lilly Endowment Inc., sponsored study, while focused on chief academic officers, examined institutional leadership and governance practices and how various constituent groups worked with the academic dean/academic vice president to achieve change. Jeanne P. McLean, *Leading from the Center: The Emerging Role of the Chief Academic Officer* (Atlanta: Scholars Press, 1999).

2. Ronald A. Heifitz, *Leadership without Easy Answers* (Cambridge, Mass.: The Belknap Press of Harvard University Press, 1994) 104–22.

3. Parker J. Palmer, *The Courage to Teach: Exploring the Inner Landscape of a Teacher's Life* (San Francisco: Jossey-Bass, 1998).

4. Ibid., 156.

5. Dietrich Bonhoeffer, *Life Together* (New York: Harper & Row, 1954) 26–27.

6. Eugene Peterson, *A Long Obedience in the Same Direction: Discipleship in an Instant Society* (Downers Grove, Ill.: Intervarsity Press, 2000).

CHAPTER 9

Reflections from the Wider Church

In writing and gathering the essays for this book on educating ministers for the church, we wanted to invite individuals to comment who have not been involved with the Keystone Conferences but who have a stake in the outcomes. We invited six people representing the wider concerns of the church to read the preceding chapters and reflect on the work accomplished, the work yet to be done, and the implications of what we have learned for the life and mission of the Christian church.

Diversity and the Challenges to Inclusion

Most Reverend Ricardo Ramírez, C.S.B.
Bishop of Las Cruces, New Mexico

The Keystone Conference and its results potentially can influence not only those involved in theological education but also the wider Catholic community in the United States. The issues theological faculties addressed as they gathered each summer—diversity, integration, and assessment—incorporate themes all church institutions in our country need to consider. I especially congratulate the participants in the Keystone Conference for the attention given to diversity. Most of my remarks will focus on this issue, mainly from a Hispanic perspective.

One of the most obvious phenomena in the country is the dramatic increase of new Hispanic immigrants into this country, especially from Mexico. The need for ordained and nonordained ministers to serve the new millions, now present in great numbers in every diocese, is urgent. Bishops are looking to Latin America and the Caribbean to recruit priests and seminarians to serve the pastoral needs of the Spanish-speaking in their dioceses. What was especially relevant at the Keystone Conferences was attention to the increase of Hispanic seminarians, most of whom are not native to the United States but are themselves immigrants. If prepared well, they will answer the prayers of not only bishops but also of their Hispanic peers. Everywhere I go in this country, I keep hearing the question, "*¿Cuándo nos van a mandar a un sacerdote mexicano?*" ("When will they send us a Mexican priest?").

What is immediately apparent to theological faculties is that there is no uniformity among Hispanic theological students. First of all, they have come from various countries, and each country has its own Spanish accent, some variations in their Spanish vocabulary, different cultural and even racial backgrounds. Most of the Hispanic students are *mestizo,* that is, a cultural and ethnic blend of Spanish and Indian backgrounds. There will be some who are not "mixed" at all and come from a purely indigenous background where the first language may not even be Spanish but an Indian one. Those with stronger indigenous backgrounds are a unique gift to our church, inasmuch as they bring a rich cultural tradition of spirituality, folklore, myths, philosophy, and a solid foundation of Catholicity. These people will be very proud of their background and may need encouragement to share their unique way of thinking and appreciating the world of the Spirit.

Hispanic seminarians bring with them a strong Catholic identity, and with their immigrant families, find comfort in a Catholic setting. In fact, the Catholic Church may be the only thing they will find in this country with which they can relate. Practically all Hispanic seminarians in this country were born into Catholic families and will be familiar with the sacramental life of the church as well as with Catholic popular devotions. There will be a strong appreciation of the Blessed Virgin Mary, especially under the title of Our Lady of Guadalupe.

Among the diverse characteristics of Hispanic theology students will be the varying degrees of acculturation to the ways of the United States, its culture, and its church. As is true of other groups, some Hispanics acculturate more quickly than others. There will also be a greater or lesser desire to acculturate or assimilate into the American way of life. Latin America shares with other parts of the world a critical view of United States foreign policy and way of life. There will be wariness or a suspicion to what they find in our theological schools, and they may wonder whether the church in the U.S. is supportive of what its government does. They will certainly be critical about our materialistic bent as well as the priority given to power and prestige.

Hospitality can be enigmatic in the mind of the Hispanic. Hispanics already belong to the church and feel that they are full members of the household of God. Some might feel perplexed as to why they are "welcomed" into what is already their home. In other words, what theological faculties and non-Hispanic peers must recognize is that Hispanic students have ownership as much as anyone else in the Catholic Church. This does not mean that hospitality is not a real issue. Seminaries have to be welcoming but never in a condescending way.

In order to be more welcoming and understanding of students from other countries or cultures, communities could be creative in planning events or celebrations to honor different cultures. These events should be more than enjoying one another's food and entertainment but should reach deep into the given culture. The entire community should know the history, the folk traditions, the literature, and musical traditions of one another's cultures.

Spiritual direction and counseling can play a pivotal role in theological education and formation of a Hispanic seminarian. The ideal is that there be available on the staff Hispanic spiritual directors and counselors. It is true that non-Hispanic spiritual directors and counselors can be just as sensitive and effective with Hispanic students as anyone else. However, these non-Hispanics will probably need special training for dealing with students coming from a culture not their own. An effective strategy is that of the *padrino-madrina* relationship. These "godparents" or "sponsors" can be invaluable persons who can accompany the theology student through formation. It might be helpful if the theology student is assigned a family that will serve in this capacity.

About twenty-five years ago, Fr. Arturo Pérez established Casa Jesús in the Archdiocese of Chicago. This house of discernment and preparation for seminary for Hispanic students still exists today and has had great success. In fact, several priests in the Archdiocese of Chicago began their seminary training at Casa Jesús. At Casa Jesús students study English and other college-level courses while they go through a period of discernment of a priestly vocation. The moderators of Casa Jesús are skilled in counseling and spiritual direction. When they are ready for theology and for a predominantly English environment, students proceed to the major seminary. Cardinal Norberto Rivera of Mexico City started a seminary for Mexicans who have discovered a possible priestly vocation while they were immigrants in the United States. These students are sent to Mexico City to pursue studies in philosophy and the English language. When they finish philosophy, they are sent to the United States to pursue their theological education. It may be too early to assess this project, but several dioceses in the United States are availing themselves of this house of formation.

Since a good number of Mexican and other Latin American seminarians have been in seminaries in their native countries, it might be a good idea for U.S. faculties to be in contact with theological faculties in Latin America. The dialogue would be helpful to the church in the North as well as the South. This might well be a way of expanding the wisdom community.

Theological schools throughout Latin America are also going through transition periods and have to deal with their own issues of diversity. Some of the Hispanic students in our U.S. schools have already studied in seminaries in Latin America; some may have even had theological training. These students will already have experienced pedagogical methods for learning theology different from what is offered in the United States. The method for case studies, for example, may be quite foreign for these students. They may also find it difficult to accept interaction between teachers and students. Some may be used to the more traditional lecture system. Some may even find writing papers strange.

One of the greatest challenges facing Hispanic students will be the ability to handle the English language. Difficulties with English can be an enormous impediment in the teaching and learning of theology. Perhaps the best approach would be not to send a Spanish-speaking student to theological studies until he has satisfactory mastery over the English language. It would be unfair for the student and for the faculty to be faced with linguistic obstacles. In some of our seminaries, it may be possible for the native Spanish-speaking student to submit papers in Spanish and also to take exams in that language.

While the focus on the diversity of theological schools is a significant contribution of this book, the chapter on "Building Communities of Wisdom" can be especially useful for the United States Catholic Conference of Bishops, for dioceses, and for parishes. It shows how to name issues by way of sharing ideas and skillful listening. It is important that the bishops of the U.S., for example, take ownership of critical issues affecting our church. We can find good advice on how to create an environment for engaging leaders on a variety of topics as we go about our committee work as a conference. We could also benefit from the principles identified in chapter 8 regarding leaders of change. In fact, the conference would be well served if we were to assess how we operate as a conference and look at ourselves from a point of view of possible adaptations of our *modus operandi*.

One of the great themes of the Second Vatican Council is that of *communio*. Communion in the Church has to happen at every level: family, parish, diocese, as well as at a national and international levels. The Keystone Conference has been an exercise in *communio*. Already it is a success insofar as the process that it used is one that embodies the essential characteristics at arriving at *communio:* identifying real issues, sharing, listening, and working together to formulate strategies that point to collaboration to deal with the challenges of our day. In a world so broken, divided, and at war, we need the church to exemplify that, in spite of diversity, we can be one and be seen as a community of wisdom.

Sending Down Roots

Kathy Brown, Director of Formation for Ministry
Washington Theological Union

Jesus uses the image of a tree bearing fruit to express what our lives as Christian disciples are meant to be (Luke 6:44-45). Those called to ministry in the church feel that call in their lives in a unique and even radical way. Their vocations as ministers bring forth the fruit of God's Kingdom here on earth, and offer life and sustenance for God's people.

Lay ministers face particular challenges as they live out their vocations. Because lay leadership is still a fairly recent reality in the modern church, lay ministers find they must earn the sacred trust of God's people. That process can be challenging and difficult as lay ministers find their credibility, competence, and even their right to minister questioned. They minister in a church where people's backgrounds, images of God, views of the church, and readiness to accept lay ministry differ widely. They frequently find themselves in situations in which there are no clear guidelines, rules, or rubrics for nonordained ministers, and where careful judgment needs to be exercised.

For all of these reasons, lay ministers need a solid ministerial identity as the "root system" from which the tree grows and brings forth its fruit. The tree reaches upward and outward toward the light, and the light brings forth life. But the tree also reaches downward into the root system that nourishes and sustains that life. The roots of a strong, healthy ministerial identity are necessarily complex, far-reaching, and continuously growing. Education for ministry in seminaries and theology schools shapes and forms the root system of ministerial identity and influences the harvest of fruit throughout the lifetime of the minister.

The church's lay ministers work in diocesan, parish, and campus communities in which there is a great diversity of needs, languages, and theological outlooks, much the same sort of diversity that Sr. Katarina Schuth describes as comprising the student body of seminaries and theology schools. The work of lay ministers in a diocesan, parish, or campus setting can be a bridge across that diversity, or it can have the opposite effect and actually increase fragmentation and polarization. If lay ministers do not honor diversity as a source of richness and strength, they can feel threatened by it, like the student Jonathan described in chapter one.

On the other hand, if lay ministers have been formed in an environment of inclusiveness that honors and even embraces diversity, they are more likely to promote unity within the Body of Christ. As they reflect upon their own experience of being "on the margins," they are more likely to respond sensitively to those who might feel outside of the mainstream. They will approach ministry with the mindset that "we are not dealing with a problem, but with people formed in a variety of ways under a variety of circumstances" (p. 2). Their response will more likely be not to try to "fix" anyone but to create hospitable, safe, and welcoming "environments in which (people's) gifts and their potential for significant service in the church can be cultivated," not to control but to empower. Approaches to theological and ministerial education that value inclusiveness and openness to a diversity of ideas are more likely to produce ministers who are open to new and different ideas, who understand faith as something dynamic rather than static, and who see that nurturing the spiritual lives of the People of God requires openness to the transformative power of the Spirit.

The complexity of ministry calls for a level of integration within the minister, which Victor Klimoski defines as "a permeability among knowledge, practice and identity." Appreciating the importance of integration can be a new and challenging way of thinking. We live in a compartmentalized world, and lay ministers who balance family, community, and professional responsibilities—like Charlene in chapter one—can easily fall into compartmentalization as a way to cope. A minister formed without recognizing the need for an integrated ministerial identity is more likely to succumb to the temptation to approach ministry as just another a job, rather than something that calls upon all of who he or she is. A minister who lacks integration is also less likely to recognize the complexity within those to whom he or she ministers —the ways in which their spiritual life permeates their everyday lives and vice versa. An approach to ministerial education that integrates theology, pastoral practice, and the prayer life of the minister models the notion that ministerial identity consists of many interconnected parts. It also recognizes that studying theology is only one part of preparing for ministry, a reality that Elizabeth, described in chapter 1, is confronting.

For a minister, identity does not come with a degree, a job, or a title as it might for someone in the business world. True ministerial identity is something that happens from the inside out. It also takes time and maturity. The permeability among knowledge, pastoral practice, and a deep, healthy spirituality begins in the heart and soul of the minister—within the root system—and flows outward. It shapes the minister's identity, worldview, and approach to ministry, opening the minister to the transforming power of grace.

Awareness of grace in a minister's spiritual life requires ongoing self-reflection in a spirit of genuine humility. When assessment is a valued and routine part of a minister's formation, that self-reflection is more likely to become a habit in his or her life and work. Regular, ongoing assessment also reinforces a desperately-needed sense of accountability on the part of the church's ministers, akin to that described in chapter 4. Ministers are called forth from the community, and part of the authority with which they minister comes from the community. In turn, a minister is accountable to the community that he or she serves.

A habit of self-reflection also keeps a minister attentive to the needs for openness to change. Ministry is engagement in a relationship with God and, like any relationship, it is a dynamic process; there is nothing static about it. The Spirit is constantly at work, calling us to conversion and transformation. Ministers need to see that not as a threat, but as a grace. In order for a tree to bear fruit, it must constantly be reaching and growing.

The tree cannot bear fruit in isolation. Its roots must reach deep into the soil, drawing life-giving water and nourishment from the earth around them. Ministry means collaborating, tapping into the wisdom and the gifts of others—peers, mentors, others in the community. The Body of Christ needs to be a community of shared wisdom, and ministers need consciously to build it into a community of shared wisdom. This need not be an extraordinary effort, but neither is it something to be taken for granted. It needs to be a habit because that is what it means to be the Body of Christ. Communities of wisdom need to be given careful attention and nurtured. There is a dynamic and creative force synergy that results from drawing on the wisdom of others. In its absence, ministers going it alone can tend to become inward focused, more concerned with their own individual success than with building the Kingdom of God. Honoring the wisdom in the wider community widens our field of vision.

The skill of attentive listening is key to forming communities of wisdom and, in fact, an essential skill for effective ministry. Kevin O'Neil asserts that the concept of building "communities of wisdom" models a way of developing the environment for ministerial education. It is a model for collaboration in which all members tap into the wisdom they share generously as members of the Body of Christ. Ministers formed in a community of wisdom will tend to seek out such communities in their work. More importantly, they may be inspired to form them where they do not yet exist.

To Inspire Conversion and Lead Change

Barry Strong, O.S.F.S., Pastor, Immaculate Conception Church
Wilmington, N.C.

The beginning of the Second Vatican Council's Decree on the Ministry and Life of Priests makes it clear that the primary task of the priest is to call together and gather the People of God, teaching, sanctifying, and leading them in such a way that they are formed into the Body of Christ and the Temple of the Holy Spirit. But in a previous decree, the same council also proclaimed the laity as active participators in the function of Christ, priest, prophet, and king. The Decree on the Apostolate of Lay People declares:

> The parish offers an outstanding example of community apostolate, for it gathers into a unity all the human diversities that are found there and inserts them into the universality of the Church (#10).

Formation for pastoral ministry in the parish setting must begin with this end in mind, that the seminarian who becomes the ordained priest and pastor as well as the lay student who becomes the lay ecclesial minister and pastoral administrator will both, in their own ways, need the requisite knowledge, skills, and attitude of heart to integrate the diversity that is the contemporary parish in matters of liturgy and service. Without it, the decree warns, the full effect of a pastor's ministry will be placed in jeopardy.

I have read the chapters of this book from my current vantage point as a pastor and as a former graduate teacher of seminarians and lay students, staff member for formation ministry, and an employee in training and organizational development. Reflecting on these essays has been a rewarding experience. The wisdom community that generated this work has confirmed and expressed my own insights into the relatedness of these topics and how they bear productively on parish life today.

The crux of pastoral ministry is the ability to inspire conversion and lead change. Sometimes we as pastoral leaders see the things that need to be developed; at other times our eyes are opened by others. In either case, we cannot do it alone. What we can do as pastoral leaders is to create an environment that invites transformation to occur within the parish on both individual and communal levels, recognizing that our parish is probably anything but like the one we grew up in and that its members resemble the same diversity of catechetical foundations and ecclesial expectations that were presented in the student profiles of chapter 1.

Chapter 8 admonishes the faculty and administration of theological centers to engage in a broad based revisiting of their mission and programs. Those who choose to do so would do well to make this process as transparent as possible to their students. It is exactly what they will need to do in the parish setting, not autocratically, but using the standard tools of needs assessment and inviting the "buy-in" of parish leadership. Transforming a loose collection of parishioners into an integrated stewardship community that owns and incarnates its parish mission will call forth the same skill set. Transforming a content driven catechetical or RCIA program into a hospitable process that takes into account the background, experience, and questions of the seeker requires a strong theological background and an openness to current research on pedagogy, adult learning styles, and the technology named in chapter 8 that one already encounters in local schools and workplace training events.

Pastoral leaders need to be able to call their pastoral councils or catechists together and invite them to envision these realities (e.g., what does this parishioner look like?), commit themselves to change, chart the course by means of goals and objectives, and assess their progress. What would happen if pastoral councils or parish staffs annually set time aside to identify the gaps that still exist between the parish mission statement and the lived reality? What if they questioned the usual practices that now seem to be ineffective? Parishes are organic realities that negotiate programmed stages of development. I affirm the insight offered in chapter 4 that the things parishes do are often the by-product of an "oral culture in which past practices tend to lead to present decisions." It can get to the point that no one quite remembers how things got to be this way. The ability to call parish leaders together to write a plan and assess progress over time is a proper expectation of the wise and faithful steward engaged in church ministry.

Pastoral leaders need to be solidly grounded in Scripture and all the disciplines of theology and pastoral care as the one to whom parishioners will turn with their questions of faith and personal problems. This is the task of the theological school. But this same minister must also be prepared to form a "local school of theology." The pastor needs to educate and transform parishioners into parish ministers and ministry coordinators. Not every pastor will have the financial wherewithal simply to hire the best for a staff position that needs filling. Dedicated parishioners will vary in their ability to perform their chosen ministry and will need theological instruction as well as coaching in order to achieve higher performance levels found in the illustration of Wiggins and McTigue's on "Aspects of Understanding" in chapter 3. The issue is one of competence, primarily on the part of the church's professional minister. At the same time the church minister also needs to foster competence in the laity who volunteer for church ministry at the parish level.

It would be naïve to think that any single program of theological-pastoral formation could provide even the most pliable candidate for the ministry with a complete set of competencies needed to function well in parish life. For that, the candidate needs to possess a commitment to lifelong learning and openness to forming intentional communities of wisdom with other pastors or pastoral administrators. The insights of chapters 6 and 7, relative to the common tasks of theological faculties, are applicable to parish leaders. A lot of pain and frustration could be avoided if, for example, a local deanery set time aside to name a few issues that were common to all parishes in the area, flesh out a case study, compare their different approaches and existing parish policies, accept feedback, and imagine and evaluate alternative ways of proceeding. How many newly ordained or first time pastors or administrators could be helped if they were given a supportive environment in which to acknowledge their "impostorship syndrome," a reality named in chapter 5.

Building a community of wisdom needs to occur within the parish too. What parish pastoral council wouldn't feel invigorated and valued for their service if the pastor led them to set aside sabbatical time to focus intentionally on the parish's deepest concerns and challenges? Adapt wisdom from Parker Palmer if we want to grow in our practice *as pastors* we have two primary places to go: to the inner ground from which good pastoring comes and to the community of fellow pastors from whom we can learn more about ourselves and our craft. The schools of theology can till the soil and plant the seeds in that inner ground. Opening oneself up to peer review requires a secure sense of self and the virtue of humility.

Ultimately, pastors and pastoral administrators need to be prepared to gather adult believers into a Catholic parish that is a vibrant part of the Body of Christ made present in the local church at the diocesan level and a church in union with that global Catholic communion of churches centered in the church of Rome. This catholicity, an essential note of the church, is by no means a static entity. It is organic and eschatological, already there yet not fully realized. At any given time on any given day, those who are gathered along with their pastor are simultaneously people who are created, fallen, graced, and called to glory. Becoming a Catholic parish is never ending. No parish, no pastor or pastoral administrator is ever finished. Becoming a Catholic parish is a dynamic reality because the parish community is never the same for long. The struggle for integrated catholicity continues with the loss or addition of each member. This is the apostolate of the parish envisioned by the Second Vatican Council.

Both Challenge and Grace

Sr. Mary C. Boys, S.N.J.M.
Skinner and McAlpin Professor of Practical Theology
Union Theological Seminary, New York City

I write these reflections just as a new academic year dawns, so the insightful recommendations of the participants of the Keystone Conference intermingle with some of my own hopes as a theological educator on the precipice of yet another school year. Although my initial readings of these chapters lead me to an appreciation of their usefulness, subsequent re-readings evoked uneasiness. Let me begin with my disquiet and then offer a few ideas that complement and develop some of the recommendations.

A Preliminary Word

My personal background will help contextualize my observations. I am a lifelong practicing Catholic, educated in Catholic schools in the Pacific Northwest for seventeen years, and I hold a doctorate from Columbia University/Union Theological Seminary where my mentor was the late, beloved Raymond E. Brown. I am a member of a religious congregation of women since 1965, with a specialty in the teaching of religion and theology. After teaching for five years in a Catholic secondary school and completing graduate study, I was on the faculty of the theology department/Institute of Religious Education and Pastoral Ministry at Boston College for seventeen years, and am beginning my eleventh year of teaching at the historically Protestant, now ecumenical Union Theological Seminary. I served for nine years on the board of trustees at a Catholic seminary in the Midwest and for two years as a consultant to the Hebrew Union College (the seminary of the Reform Movement of Judaism). Over the course of the last twenty years, I have had increasing involvement in Christian-Jewish dialogue where my research and writing in the past decade has been principally focused. My involvement in the ecumenical and interreligious arena has immeasurably enriched my Catholicism.

The Love of Learning and the Desire for God

In his brilliant study of monastic culture, Jean Leclercq depicts a time and place when piety and study were inextricably linked (*The Love of Learning and the Desire for God,* Fordham University Press, 1982). It presents an ideal for every age, one ours sorely needs—and our seminaries in particular.

As delighted as I was to see emphasis on the art and craft of teaching at the Keystone Conferences, various references to students who are unwilling to "engage in the learning enterprise because of preconceived ideas about theology they do not wish to change" (p. 37) gave me pause. That nearly ten percent of the seminarians can be described as having a "rigid understanding of faith," who "think of themselves as invariably right in their views about the Church" and find "any new insight . . . a threat," seeing "things through a single lens" and un-interested "in discussion or dialogue" (p. 42) is truly a cause for lament. That seminarians *resist* historical-critical methods of biblical study despite the profound work of renowned Catholic and Protestant biblical scholars is further cause for worry. The rigid personality described here suggests a fundamentalist worldview; when combined with zeal, it contributes to further polarization and complicates the church's role in the public square. When such seminarians and lay students persist in their refusal to learn beyond their narrow ideological confines, they manifest inaptitude for ministry.

Beyond this group, however, is a larger question of what contemporary Catholic culture reveals about the connection of learning to the life of faith. On the North American landscape, anti-intellectualism in the religious sphere has long been an issue; witness the learned minister controversy in the eighteenth-century that continued into the Second and Third Great Awakenings (1800–1830 and 1890–1920, respectively). Anti-intellectual tendencies in U.S. Roman Catholic life were in part a result of the vast numbers of relatively unschooled immigrants who poured onto these shores between 1840 and 1920. Perhaps all of us would be wise to revisit the discussion elicited in the mid-1950s by John Tracy Ellis's, *American Catholics and the Intellectual Life* (Heritage Foundation, Inc., 1956).

It is difficult to discern much leadership these days from the hierarchy in regard to learning in the service of truth for the sake of transformation. Indeed, it seems in too many dioceses that the issues raised by the sexual abuse crisis have so preoccupied the bishops that little time and energy is left for their own study. Moreover, a culture has developed among the U.S. bishops in which differences are suppressed and debate hidden. Peter Steinfels claims that, in being "careful to a fault about what they say and do," the bishops have sacrificed "the kind of honest debate and respectful but frank disagreement that brings pressing issues to the forefront and opens them to analysis" (*A People Adrift: The Crisis in the Roman Catholic Church in America*, Simon and Schuster, 2003, p. 346).

Admittedly, my sensitivities to the way in which study is too little prized in Catholicism today are heightened by my involvement in Christian-Jewish dialogue. Study plays a prominent role in Jewish life. When the Jews I know gather, they virtually always open their meeting with some sort of study session. From very early years, Jewish children are encouraged to ask questions and to develop a curiosity that fuels learning. Perhaps the Jewish writer Chaim Potok expresses this commitment most eloquently. In his novel *In the Beginning* (Alfred A. Knopf, 1975), one of the characters, Rav Sharfman, says to his pupil David Lurie, "A shallow mind is a sin against God" (p. 424).

One of the great challenges of theological education today is to enable students to discover that the love of learning can deepen desire for God and, concomitantly, that desire for God can arouse passion for learning.

Learning to Listen, Learning to Teach

One of the Keystone Conference recommendations that comes through most clearly is the importance of listening in theological education— that sort of deep listening attuned to cultural sensitivities, learning style differences, life experiences, and theological perspectives. I believe that we might learn much wisdom from educational "experts," especially from those like Jane Vella and Stephen Brookfield who are so clearly attentive to their own craft. I believe the implementation of recommendations of the Keystone Conferences will be both advanced and enhanced by drawing upon a number of useful works. Let me briefly recommend several books I believe are foundational to putting the recommendations found here into practice.

The works of Stephen Brookfield belong on the bookshelf of every seminary and school of ministry. I would put his *The Skillful Teacher* (Jossey-Bass, 1990) into the hands of every new faculty member, and make his *Discussion as a Way of Teaching* (Jossey-Bass, 1999) a central element of faculty meetings over the course of the academic year. This latter book may even inspire a conversion in those who regard discussion as "shared ignorance" that detracts from lecturing. Brookfield's chapter on "Keeping Discussion Going Through Questioning, Listening, and Responding" offers a wealth of ideas, as does the chapter on "Discussion in Culturally Diverse Classrooms." An excellent complement to Brookfield from a more philosophical perspective is *Dialogue in Teaching* (Teachers College Press, 1993) by Nicholas Burbules.

The increased attention to diversity in race, ethnicity, class, gender, and culture is an important development in our time. Among the many works now available on issues of diversity is a profoundly personal and insightful work by my former colleague Kathleen Talvacchia, *Critical Minds and Discerning Hearts* (Chalice Press, 2003). Talvacchia organizes her arguments around Brookfield's notion of "critical incidents," recounting and analyzing crises in her own educational work. Cognitive psychologist Howard Gardner offers another vantage point on diversity with his theory of "multiple intelligences" in *Intelligence Reframed: Multiple Intelligences for the 21st Century* (Basic Books, 1999). If intelligence is, as Gardner argues, a "biopsychological potential to process information that can be activated in a cultural setting to solve problems that are of value in a culture," then it is vital to move beyond the usual equation of linguistic and logical-mathematical skills as the primary (or only) markers of intelligence (pp. 33–34). Gardner argues that in addition to those two "intelligences," we also consider at least five other "intelligences": bodily-kinesthetic, spatial, musical, interpersonal, and intrapersonal. Many educators have taken up Gardner's work, and theological educators would do well to follow their lead.

Jane Vella's *Learning to Listen, Learning to Teach: The Power of Dialogue in Educating Adults* (Jossey-Bass, 2002) is an immensely useful and engaging book. Because Vella has taught all over the world, she has well-developed cultural sensitivities and uses her global experiences to illustrate what she terms "twelve principles for effective adult learning." Her work offers specific ways to move from probing the needs of learners to formulating tasks that will meet those needs.

I write the concluding words of this reflection just hours after teaching my first class of the semester. The frenetic pace of the beginnings gives way to reflection on all that happened in the three hours of class —an invitation to contemplate, one of the most important aspects of the pedagogical process as noted by Marget Buchmann in *The Careful Vision: How Practical Is Contemplation in Teaching?* (The National Center for Research on Teacher Education at Michigan State University, 1989). To pay attention, to listen, to hear God speaking even in the sounds of sheer silence (the NRSV translation of 1 Kings 19:12), that is the keystone of the educational process.

A Truly Ecumenical Enterprise

Raymond Williams, Founding Director
Wabash College for Teaching and Learning in Theology and Religion
Professor Emeritus, Department of Religion, Wabash College

It is appropriate that Roman Catholic theological teachers take the lead in developing an ecumenical wisdom about teaching and learning. "Catholic" in the designation implies that they deal with the major issues in contemporary experience, both religious and secular: diversity, integration, accountability, technology, constructive leadership, and effective pedagogy. Nothing proves more effectively that Roman Catholic theological schools are not ivory towers isolated from the current social realities than the reflection about teaching and learning displayed in this book. The issues are complex and the challenges pressing, so this gift of practical wisdom is for the whole church and the world.

The wisdom of the teachers of the church cannot be imposed upon others; it must always be a gift of good news and grace. Two propositions undergird the thesis that the best of Roman Catholic thinking and practice in teaching and learning can be a universal gift valuable to the whole church and to the world.

The first proposition is that some form of teaching and learning is central to all creative human relationships, from the earliest formation of children by parents to the most complex relationships of adults in human institutions. It is essential to survival. Word and communication are constitutive of humanity, and teaching and learning form primary modes of communication. Humans have a unique ability to create, manipulate, and transmit symbols and symbol systems of great complexity and high abstraction. That ability necessitates lengthy nurturing and socialization and also increasing specialization. Thus, teaching and learning are very close to the essential character of humanity as its basic social ontology. The communal aspect of all living and working is the reason for the basic injunction of good teaching stressed in this book—"Know your students." The implication is that each student is a distinct individual, and a class of students is uniquely shaped by diverse social contexts. Interactive engagement and understanding are essential for facilitating creative relationships. Because the communication inherent in good teaching and learning is constitutive of our basic humanity, theological teachers bear a special responsibility to share the best thinking and best practice with the entire church and other human institutions.

The second proposition is that theological reflection on formation is an aspect of the deepest human desire for meaning and purpose. It is teleological, dealing with the goal and end of human life and society. Attention to integration enhances coherence of an individual's vocation and sharpens a focus on an institution's mission. Some people may not use theological language or frameworks in describing human formation and meaning or in creating the most effective strategies for promoting positive development. Nevertheless, wisdom developed by Roman Catholic theological teachers regarding formation can be instructive to others in creating and reaching a clearer vision of the effective person, healthy church, and civil society.

A reason for the ecumenical relevance of this book is that the three central issues of diversity, integration, and assessment facing Roman Catholics are universal. New and increased diversity in every social institution of American life results from recent immigration and is generated by intricate transnational networks. A result is that previous assumptions about norms, procedures, and goals are being reformulated in an exciting and creative period in American life. Because religion is a powerful force in establishing personal and group identity, especially for recent immigrants, current negotiation of diverse groups promises to be formative for American church and society. That is one reason why integration is a central issue. Integration implies a worldview that provides coherence to personal and group identity as an American, as a Christian, and in a specialized role in society. How one educates or socializes individuals and groups into coherent and creative identities is one of the greatest contemporary challenges in both church and society. The attempt of institutions to establish clear goals to fulfill their respective missions and to be accountable in their stewardship of religious and social resources requires ongoing assessment of their processes and results.

Teachers and administrators of Protestant theological schools meeting in the Lexington Seminars, a program analogous to the Keystone project, raise the same critical issues of diversity, integration, and assessment that challenge Roman Catholic theological education. Hence, Protestants are able to draw from these chapters the best thinking and practice of Roman Catholic theological teachers. For instance, theological integration, as defined by Victor Klimoski in this book as "a formative process that engages students in traditions of theological knowledge, pastoral practice, and Christian identity as they examine, reinterpret, and commit themselves to a worldview that bears the deep imprint of those traditions" (p. 50), is equally challenging for Protestant seminaries. This book reflects how the Catholic bishops' authoritative *Program of Priestly Formation* influences the way programs and their structures bear the imprint of a singular vision. Protestant theological education has no such document. At the same time, Protestant theological educators working in the Lexington Seminars also contribute to this ecumenical discussion which is captured in the book *Practical Wisdom: On Theological Teaching and Learning* (Peter Lang, 2004). The perspectives raised there can augment and expand how Catholic seminary and theological faculties envision their work in service of the church.

A claim to catholicity brings responsibility to do the best thinking and to engage in the best practices regarding important matters for the whole church and the whole world. That is a daunting challenge incumbent upon Roman Catholic theological teachers and schools. Authors of chapters in this book take up the challenge and reflect for us the best thinking and the most pressing concerns of a broad spectrum of Catholic schools. Although the result found here is firmly grounded in contemporary local realities, it is neither sectarian nor provincial. Wisdom about theological teaching has catholic and ecumenical application beyond Roman Catholic theological schools. It is a truly ecumenical gift.

In the end, theological schools exist because of the church, for the church nurtures students for ministry, and most Roman Catholic and mainline Protestant churches depend on the seminaries for people prepared for pastoral leadership. Thus, churches and theological schools have an intimate relationship and mirror each other. Diversity in the churches appears in the schools. The need for integration of life and work with a mature faith challenges congregations and their members seeking to live as faithful Christians just as students and their faculties strive for a similar integration. Unfortunately, congregations, church agencies, and individual Christians rarely focus on integration and even more rarely develop sophisticated means for assessing their faithfulness and effectiveness. As authors in this book have indicated, strategies developed in the schools regarding diversity, integration, and assessment are adaptable for congregations and agencies of the church.

Theological schools and the church together exist for the world. This shared focus can foster the best thinking and development of the best practices as we seek to embrace contemporary diversity, to develop new paths toward integration of life and work, and to strive for greater mission effectiveness and relevance by engaging strategies of accountability. These are tasks which theological schools are uniquely equipped to examine critically and, in dialogue with the church, to prepare its pastors for creative, effective leadership.

Facing the Deeper Questions

Peter Steinfels, Religion Editor, New York Times
and Author, A People Adrift:
The Crisis of the Roman Catholic Church in America

I cannot overstate how much I admire the dedication and thoughtfulness of the Keystone Conferences as reflected in this book. Two of the challenges that participants highlighted—the integration of course work into life-shaping knowledge, wisdom, and habits of learning, and the need for continually assessing the whole educational experience—confront educators at every level of schooling. The third challenge, diversity among students, while not quite as universal, is quickly becoming so.

I have confronted all three challenges in teaching college undergraduates and, most recently, in teaching students of theology and pastoral ministry. I could have profited—I hope that I will profit—not only from the ideas about pedagogy revealed in this book but from the profound spiritual wisdom that often informs and accompanies them. Not a few passages were humbling in the most useful of ways.

There is a standard joke about prison reform that probably has its echo in discussions of seminary and theological education: The key to prison reform, it is often quipped, is getting a better class of inmates. What is impressive about these chapters is the determination of the Keystone Conference participants to avoid that kind of reaction. They do not treat students as a problem in need of "fixing"; they accept the complex reality of their current student bodies and strive to create effective learning environments in recognition of this reality. They take on the responsibility of change rather than shift it elsewhere, whether to the students, the church, or society at large.

Seminary and theological educators are not usually considered at the forefront of educational change. But I am not sure that the willingness signaled here to rethink and rework instructional approaches, curriculum design, the use of new technology, and the tools of assessments—all in pursuit of nothing less than creating genuine communities of wisdom—would be matched in most other sectors of higher education.

Those are my reactions as a sometime teacher who has been intensely involved in discussions of the potential of Catholic higher education and the problems to be faced in fulfilling that potential. They are also my reactions as a Catholic worried about the church's present and future leadership. I hope that the approaches articulated during the

Keystone Conferences invigorate Catholic theological and seminary education.

As a worried Catholic I have another reaction, however. I worry that the Conferences' admirable determination to take their students as they are and address their needs hasn't set aside too many questions about the qualifications of these students in the first place.

I am struck by the nearly total absence of discussion of issues of sexuality among candidates for ordination. The description of students offered here says nothing about being gay or heterosexual or about the place of sexual identity, sexual experience, or considerations of marriage in their discernment of a vocation. I cannot believe that, in terms of the challenges posed by diversity, these factors are not as consequential as some that are stressed here.

Likewise, while not retracting anything I have said about the importance of faculty members' efforts to respond creatively to the intellectual characteristics of the students in front of them, I am uneasy about treating those characteristics as a form of diversity that should be accepted matter-of-factly or even welcomed much as one does ethnic or cultural differences.

"Though much has been said about educational levels of students, few current statistical studies are available," Sr. Katarina Schuth reports. I want to ask, why not? A plethora of quantitative data about the scores on various tests are available for many other fields and individual institutions. Indeed, many schools make a point of publicizing this material; schools that do not are generally willing to make it available to researchers to amalgamate with other data. Such information does not measure as much as people sometimes suppose, but at least it provides a relatively objective indicator of trends. The fact that it is lacking for seminarians and theological students—or not available even to a leading researcher—makes me wonder whether in fact church officials would prefer that the trends not be measured or, if measured, not be known. If assessment is desirable, as the Keystone conferees argue, surely it includes standard statistical studies like these.

The guesstimates that the conferees must supply in the absence of that data are not reassuring. Ten percent of the students in their institutions are "highly qualified." Some forty percent "experience one or more learning difficulties" and "this last group creates special challenges for faculty." I realize that this forty percent includes a significant number, like those for whom English is not a native language, whose learning difficulties might be relatively easily reparable, but then there is the overlapping category, including some among the academically well qualified as well as among the academically deficient, who "regardless of native abilities and educational experiences" resist "the learning enterprise" because it threatens their "preconceived ideas about theology."

These impressions are, in fact, widely shared, perhaps to the point that they have lost all power to disturb. What if it were reported that only ten percent of those studying for medical degrees were academically or intellectually "highly qualified"? Or that forty percent of those accepted for law school or graduate degrees in engineering labored under one or more learning difficulties creating "special challenges for faculty?" Or that, well-equipped or not for their studies, some significant percentage of those in medicine, law, engineering, social work, education, or for that matter the military, displayed an "unwillingness . . . to engage in the learning enterprise" that they were undergoing? One hardly need add that in fields like medicine, law, and engineering, there are both state required exams and market pressures to weed out the unqualified, while in matters of church leadership there seem to be neither.

The sensitivity of those responsible for seminary and theological education to the ethnic and cultural diversity and their openness to the fact that the students of today are not the students of four decades ago must be applauded. But those positive developments should not eclipse the responsibility, not only of educators but all concerned Catholics, to press questions about the pool of students from which so many of the church's key leaders, ordained and lay, will be drawn.

Index